MANNA & MYSTERY

MANNA & MYSTERY

A Jungian Approach to Hebrew Myth and Legend

Bettina L. Knapp

Foreword by Murray Stein

Chiron Publications • Wilmette, Illinois

Chiron Publications acknowledges the following for their permissions.

The Golem, pp. 38–61, is an extract from the original that appeared in Bettina L. Knapp, *The Prometheus Syndrome*, Whitston Press, 1979, pp. 97–130, Copyright © 1979 by Whitston Press. Reprinted by permission of the publisher.

The Dybbuk, pp. 62–96, is an extract from the original that appeared in Bettina L. Knapp, *Theater and Alchemy*, Wayne State University Press, 1980, pages 154–186, Copyright © 1980 by Wayne State University. Reprinted by permission of the publisher.

"Edo and Anam," pp. 120–139, originally appeared in Bettina L. Knapp, *Exile and the Writer*, University Park: The Pennsylvania State University Press, 1991, pp. 111–129, Copyright © 1991 by The Pennsylvania State University. Reproduced by permission of the publisher.

Chart on p. 99 is from Gershom Scholem, *Major Trends in Jewish Mysticism*, Jerusalem: Schocken Publishing House, 1941, Copyright © 1941 by Schocken Publishing House, Reprinted by permission of Schocken Books, published by Pantheon Books, a division of Random House, Inc.

Library of Congress Catalog Card Number: 94–3553

Printed in the United States of America.
Copyedited by Susan C. Roberts.
Book design by Siobhan Drummond.
Cover design by D. J. Hyde.

Library of Congress Cataloging-in-Publication Data:

Knapp, Bettina Liebowitz, 1926–
    Manna and mystery : a Jungian approach to Hebrew myth and legend / Bettina L. Knapp : foreword by Murray Stein.
        p.   cm.
    Includes bibliographical references and index.
    ISBN 0-933029–80-2 : $16.95
    1. Legends, Jewish—History and criticism. 2. Jewish literature—History and criticism. 3. Archetype (Psychology) in literature.
I. Title.
BM530.K575   1995
296.1′9—dc20   94–3553
                                                                          CIP
ISBN 0–933029–80–2

Contents

Foreword

In this rich and fascinating work, Bettina Knapp has extended an ancient tradition of hermeneutics. Reflecting upon various tales, images, and human figures from Jewish myth and legend, she renders their themes instructive and meaningful for contemporary men and women. For her hermeneutical tool, she uses Jung's psychological theory and his famous "method of amplification." The results are highly rewarding.

From the viewpoint of Jungian studies and scholarship, which is my own specialty, this work is particularly welcome. Jungians have traditionally (and by now we can speak of a Jungian tradition) favored Greek and Egyptian mythologies over the biblical one, as they have also turned to Eastern religions for wisdom rather than mining more deeply what are, in most cases, their own background religions. In recent years this has begun to change, and more works such as this one by Knapp are sure to appear in the coming decade. This "new direction" is actually a return to Jung's own works of reflection on the biblical tradition and on Western religions, as exemplified in his late works *Aion* and *Answer to Job*.

Like Jung's work, too, Knapp's text is widely inclusive of materials that help render a figure or image intelligible from a symbolic and psychological point of view. What this does is give the modern reader not only information of a fascinating kind but also access to personal meaning. Her account of what it means to create a golem, for example, is both precise with respect to history and a cultural *Sitz im Leben* and also useful for understanding a universal psychic mechanism of compensation that applies as much in our lives today as it did in sixteenth-century Prague. The fascination with creating artificial intelligence today and the wonders of robotics that it promises for our future are extensions of ancient ambitions to create and command like God and to guarantee our security and well-being. Who has not enjoyed such a wild day-dream? And those who study their night dreams will also find this theme occurring spontaneously from time to time.

The highest value of a work like this one is that it opens for modern consciousness doors to ancient insight and wisdom. Not more technological knowledge but more soul gnosis is what we need today. What has occurred to humans in the modern world—whether it is called modern or post-modern is a distinction without a difference, in my opinion—is a tragic loss of soul-consciousness. More and more the external world, with its fascination and demands for attention, has monopolized the individual's consciousness. Bombarded from the world around us with messages and images, cries for help, seductions to spend or to give or to love, we have little time or energy in reserve to enter what has traditionally been called the spiritual world, the invisible world, the inner world. The inner world of subjectivity remains but a vestige of humanity, a point of reactivity, of emotionality, of irrationality. The individual's inner consciousness is rapidly approaching extinction even while it is being forced to contain more and more content from every corner of the earth. Beneath this weight of externality the individual's capacity for internal exploration is crushed. It is the mission of depth psychology to retrieve the sense of soul culturally as it is the task of depth psychotherapy to help individuals develop their own awareness of soul. Surely in our time this is the treasure lost in the field. The soul awaits our retrieval.

Knapp's work points a way toward finding the treasure of subjectivity and soulfulness. We who labor in this mission salute her.

—Murray Stein

Introduction

*The Lord gave the word: great was the
company of those that published it.
(Psalm 68:11)*

The word—the Book—was one of ancient Israel's contributions to literature, to learning, and to spirituality. Religious texts—the Bible, the Talmud, the Mishnah, apocryphal writings such as the Book of Enoch and kabbalistic works such as the *Zohar*—were and are storehouses of untold riches. Whether the above-mentioned written works take the form of short stories, proverbs, fables, parables, chronicles, dramas, poetry, myths, or legends, they may be experienced as documents of the mind, the psyche, and the soul.

In addition to sacred texts, which generate spiritual and visceral excitement, Hebrew writings throughout the centuries include philosophical texts, such as Maimonides' (Moses ben Maimon) *Guide for the Perplexed*, mystically oriented poetry, *Praise unto the Righteous* by Moses H. Luzzatto, and dramatic works. Not only did the many religious and lay tracts provide readers with sources of knowledge, they triggered the *numinosum*: those feelings and sensations that emerge when one experiences *mystery*.

The varieties of human emotion authors kindled in their readers were imbricated in the very structure of their pieces. Plot lines, nature descriptions, dialogue and narrative sequences, the actions and reactions of the protagonists, and the complex interplay of colorations and rhythmic arrangements reveal a whole inner climate. Subliminal meanings are also embedded in figures of speech used by authors: symbols, images, metaphors, repetitions, alliterations, metonymies, and so forth may serve to clarify some of the obscure or outerworldly happenings garnishing their texts.

Dreams, visions, hallucinations, synchronistic experiences, and the déja vu emanating from an author's unconscious are also interwoven into the body of literary pieces, pointing up and helping to solve problematic situations or simply to permit a cathartic outpouring of sorrow or joy.

The six works chosen for inclusion in *Manna and Mystery: A Jungian Approach to Hebrew Myth and Legend* are both mythical and legendary in quality and impact. The word *legend* (from the Latin, *legendus*, meaning "to gather, select"; and akin to the Greek, *legein*, "to gather, say") suggests a story handed down from past generations and regarded by the populace as an unverifiable historical event.

Legend in many cases is used interchangeably with myth. About myth, C. G. Jung writes:

> The collective unconscious—so far as we can say anything about it at all—appears to consist of mythological motifs or primordial images, for which reason the myths of all nations are its real exponents. In fact, the whole of mythology could be taken as a sort of projection of the collective unconscious. We can see this most clearly if we look at the heavenly constellations, whose originally chaotic forms were organized through the projection of images. This explains the influence of the stars as asserted by astrologers. These influences are nothing but unconscious, introspective perceptions of the activity of the collective unconscious. Just as the constellations were projected into the heavens, similar figures were projected into legends and fairy tales or upon historical persons. We can therefore study the collective unconscious in two ways, either in mythology or in the analysis of the individual. (1960, par. 325)

The "myth" is to be understood as the narration of a primordial experience, not necessarily personal but rather transcendental. It is not something invented for the sake of entertainment, although it may be also that, but rather a living and burning reality that exists in the psyche and culture of a people (Harding 1975, p. 268). A myth is ectypal (it deals with the existential world) and archetypal (it deals with eternal experiences). Existence on these two levels contains past, present, and future within its structure (Eliade 1963, pp. 9ff). A myth, then, lives outside of temporal time. Not bound within the limits of eschatological, linear, or historical time, it flows in a cyclical, sacred, or eternal dimension. Myth time, therefore, is reversible. The events narrated in such myths as those of the golem or the dybbuk, for example, are perpetual; they were not only understood according to the cultural canon of the time when they were written or spoken, but for some individuals and groups encompass all eras—from ancient to modern times. In that the myth is ectypal, it reveals and relives a structure or level of reality. It may then become the model or the prototype of the period or periods that brought it into being, even while reflecting, in its many transformations and recountings throughout the centuries, the needs, obsessions, and longings of other cultures.

The word *myth* stems from the Greek, *muthos*, "fable"; a myth relates a fabulous event or events. In that the time factor in the myth transcends linear time, the events narrated are experienced in a kind of eternity; in that they tell a *fable*, they may depict the "fabulous" lives of divinities, heroes, and supernatural beings. They are endowed with a religious quality because they deal with gods and extraterrestrial figures. "Religious" must be understood here in the sense of *religio* (Latin, "linking back"). Individuals identifying with certain elements of the myth are in effect sharing in the divine events and peripeteia, becoming integrated and rooted into the world of heroes and gods just as they are into theirs. Thus they are removed from their circumscribed and individual frames of reference and plunged into a collective experience. They participate in the birth of a hero or a theophany, thus helping solve a difficult or critical situation (Eliade 1963, pp. 14ff).

Myths cannot be understood merely on an intellectual level if they are to be experienced as fully as possible. Although they may arouse the ear with their poetry, the imagination with the exciting events recounted, the inner eye with their remarkable imagery, they also exist as *praxis* ("action") in the workaday world. For example, the hero in Rabbi Nachman's tale, and the struggle he endured to achieve his goal, may elicit certain emotions and attitudes in the reader identifying with him and his society. In such cases, the myth answers a specific need in the individual and perhaps in the collective, playing as it does a subtle role in the formulation of an ethos. Yentl's incredible thirst for learning in I. B. Singer's tale might imbue a woman in today's world with the stoic power necessary to pursue the specific course that she might have otherwise considered impossible. The golem myth may give a persecuted people the wisdom to forge ahead, thereby transcending oppressive existential situations. Indeed, in many cases, such as in the golem myth, the events dramatized may lend continuity to life and order to disorder while also making comprehensible that which surpasses an individual's understanding. Considered symbolically, myth may give purpose to lives that might otherwise have been considered absurd or without a raison d'être.

Each culture has its own myths and legends, which are frequently adaptations of others. Many, therefore, have common markings. For the Hebrews and for other groups throughout the world and from time immemorial, myths revolving around the New Year's celebration, for example, give the individual and the collective the impression of beginning life anew yearly. Individuals as well as the collective gain the illusion of being able to rework their lives. Similarly, the Passover feast is significant to the Hebrews, for example, not only replaying a people's escape from bondage, but also teaching them the reasons behind the ordeal of the desert experience, leading directly as it did to their rebirth in a new land. The same may be said of the myth of the "divine child" which is also implicit in many cultures and optimistic in emphasis; Moses for the Jew, Christ for the Christian, Dionysus-Iacchus for the Greeks, Horus for the Egyptian, Buddha for the Buddhist. To admire or worship a child fills the believer with the glow of hope: he—like a Messiah—will cure humanity of its ills.

Although the myths and legends chosen for scrutiny in *Manna and Mystery* deal with a variety of themes pertinent to the societies and cultures conceiving them, they also—as is the case of any living myth—may impact in many ways on today's world.

The medieval tale, "The Rabbi Who Was Turned into a Werewolf," points up a conflictual situation between the shadow, anima, and animus. So searing is the struggle between the protagonists, namely husband and wife, that real and imaginative animals have to be called into the happenings to point toward a *modus vivendi*. Indeed, associations between this medieval work and the biblical legend of Balaam (Numbers 22–24) help explain some of the enigmas involved.

"The Golem: A Recipe for Survival" discusses Chayim Bloch's retelling of one of the great myths of all time, a product of the Hebrew mystical experience. Rabbi Judah Loew, the creator of the golem ("a shapeless mass"), was motivated to accomplish his daring feat to help the Jewish community of sixteenth-century Prague survive seemingly endless bouts of religious persecution. The golem, a product of ecstatic mysticism, entered the real world as a kind of messianic figure in a time of need. Psychologically, Rabbi Loew was allowing a projection from his inner world to exist as a psychic reality. It was the golem's function to discover the plans afoot for the persecution of Jews. After he accomplished his goal and the bloodbaths diminished, Rabbi Loew withdrew the projection, reducing the golem to dust, thereby preventing people from becoming dependent on this figure. As a crystallization of an archetype, the golem could have mesmerized the entire Jewish community, thus diminishing the consciousness and aggressiveness needed to cope with the harrowing existential experiences that faced them.

"*The Dybbuk*: An Alchemical Spagyric Marriage" also concerns a tale that is mythical in scope. Indeed, Shloyme Ansky's play is a religious mystery, dealing with the drama of possession and eternal love. Leah and Channon, the protagonists of *The Dybbuk*, live in a celestial *coniunctio*. Both are carriers of *mystery*. For the kabbalist, such a union represents superior love—a spiritual rather than a temporal relationship between boy and girl. For the psychologist, it may be tantamount to a rejection of life or a living death. Whatever the interpretation, the psychic suffering and passion of the protagonists lead to a transfiguration, a kind of apotheosis.

The Rabbi Nachman story, "The Loss of the Princess," may be viewed as a homiletic tale conveying a spiritual as well as a psychological message. The princess, if approached in kabbalistic terms, may be understood as the *Shekinah*, a manifestation of the community of Israel as well as the feminine element within God himself. Psychologically, she is a representation of soul or *anima*. The "loss" of the princess after her departure from her father's kingdom ushers in a whole—and breathtaking—theory concerning God's creation of the world that is at variance with the one depicted in Genesis. As enunciated by the sixteenth-century writer Isaac Luria, this revolutionary belief states that the coming into being of the world resulted from a withdrawal of the Godhead into Himself rather than from an expansion of His powers into space. Psychologically, such an inner flow of energy replicates the human condition of introversion instead of the extroversion implied in the outward flow of libido depicted in Genesis.

"Agnon's 'Edo and Enam': An Archaeological Exploration of the Soul/Psyche" explores an S. Y. Agnon tale relating the fascinating spiritual and psychological drama confronting a young bride, Gemulah, who had left the land of her ancestors to follow her husband to Jerusalem. Descendents of one of the ten lost tribes of Israel, this Hebrew group had lived ever since biblical times in a remote mountain region, perhaps someplace in southeast Asia. A variety of happenings occur in Agnon's spellbinding mythical work: Jerusalem is experienced as an archetype of the Self; the house becomes a representative of containment and imprisonment; the two wandering scholars who seek out Gemulah, one a thinking type and the other a feeling type, are in search of ancient lost languages. Somnambulistic happenings and the occult power of the moon on the protagonists are also probed.

"I. B. Singer's 'Yentl the Yeshivah Boy': The Talmud and Gender Deconstruction" looks at Singer's dramatization of a young girl's dilemma in nineteenth-century Poland as she attempts to break out of an ultrapatriarchal society. A thinking type, she discovers ways to remain true to her nature throughout her ordeals. For some, she is considered the prototype of today's woman. Like the biblical Deborah, Yentl is possessed of remarkable resolve and steadfastness. In that she accepts psychological pain and stands her ground— paradigms of her indomitable will—she brings to mind Job's assertion to God: "Though He slay me, yet will I trust in Him: but I will maintain my own ways before Him" (Job 13–15).

The works probed in *Manna and Mystery* will, it is hoped, acquaint readers with certain literary as well as intellectual and psychological aspects of Jewish thought, life, and religious experience. As written in the *Zohar*:

"In the beginning" [Genesis 1:1]—when the will of the King began to take effect, he engraved signs into the heavenly sphere [that surrounded him]. Within the most hidden recess a dark flame issued from the mystery of the *en-sof*, the Infinite, like a fog forming in the unformed—enclosed in the ring of that sphere, neither white nor black, neither red nor green, of no color whatever. Only after this flame began to assume size and dimension did it produce radiant colors. From the innermost center of the flame sprang forth a well out of which colors issued and spread upon everything beneath, hidden in the mysterious hiddenness of *en-sof*. (Scholem 1963, p. 27)

Bibliography

Baynes, H. G. 1969. *Mythology of the Soul*. London: Rider and Company.

Buber, M. 1956. *The Tales of Rabbi Nachman*. Translated by M. Friedman. New York: Horizon Press.

Band, A. J., trans. 1978. *Nahman of Bratslav* by Rabbi Ben Simhah Nachman. New York: Paulist Press.

Eliade, M. 1963. *Aspects du mythe*. Paris: Gallimard.

Harding, E. 1975. *The Way of All Women*. New York: Harper and Row.

Jung, C. G. 1960. *The Structure and Dynamics of the Psyche*. *CW*, vol. 8. Princeton, N.J.: Princeton University Press, 1969.

Schaya, L. 1973. *The Universal Meaning of the Kabbalah*. New York: Penguin.

Scholem, G. 1965. *Major Trends in Hebrew Mysticism*. New York: Schocken Books.

———. 1973. *On the Kabbalah and Its Symbolism*. Translated by R. Manheim. New York: Schocken Books.

Scholem, G., ed. 1963. *Zohar: The Book of Splendor*. New York: Schocken Books.

"The Rabbi Who Was Turned into a Werewolf "

The Medieval Shadow/
Anima /Animus at Work

"The Rabbi Who Was Turned into a Werewolf," one of many medieval stories dating back to the tenth and twelfth centuries and preserved in both Hebrew and Yiddish, was included in *The Ma'aseh Book* of 1516. Fanciful rather than realistic, its significance is not only psychological but cultural. An exploration of the dichotomy existing between an actual life experience and the superimposition of an imaginative situation, its *dramatis personae* are projections of a fundamental incompatibility between husband and wife, as actuated in a warring shadow/anima/animus confrontation (Gaster 1981, pp. 19–33).

In keeping with biblical tradition, many of the poetic tales in *The Ma'aseh Book* were intended as learning devices. Replete with allegories and parables, some were based on the enunciations of the prophet Nathan (2 Samuel 12:1 ff), others on those of the king of Israel, Jehoash (2 Kings, 14:9 ff), or on the Proverbs of Solomon. "The Rabbi Who Was Turned into a Werewolf" bears an affinity with the tale of Balaam (Numbers 22:24).

Edifying biblical stories and parables were recounted to the faithful during the Middle Ages and thereafter, particularly at festival periods. Many homiletic tales offering practical lessons were also included in sermons delivered in the synagogues, as well as in school lessons and at home. Certain happenings in the past, be they historical or religiously oriented, could, it was believed, teach moral and spiritual values to the young and the not so young. Lives could

thereby be transformed and difficult situations turned into beneficial and meaningful ones. In that both Jews and Christians adhered
to these traditional notions, mention might be made of the *Exempla*
of Jacques de Vitry (d. 1240) or the *Golden Legends* of Jacobus
Voragine (1230–98).

Although "The Rabbi Who Was Turned into a Werewolf" is
Judaic in concept, contemporary literary and cultural influences
permeate the events enacted. According to some scholars, its param-
eters were drawn from *Bisclavret*, a medieval tale by the thirteenth-
century author Marie de France. Her Breton *Lais*, verse narrative
romances replete with Celtic lore and Arthurian material, were well
known and popular at court, as was her *Ysopet* cycle, based on the
writings of the Greek fabulist Aesop (620–560 B.C.E.). These and
other legends and tales were also sung by minnesingers, for their
wisdom as well as for their value as entertainment. Let us note that
French tales, the *fabliaux*, frequently ribald and scurrilous, featuring humanized animals, were also counted and recounted much to
the delight of popular audiences.

Rather than featuring a courtly gentleman who was turned into
an animal, as was the case in *Bisclavret*, the protagonists of "The
Rabbi Who Was Turned into a Werewolf" were a Hasidic rabbi and
his wife: the former transformed into a werewolf and the latter into
a donkey. Although some critics label the fable a "fantasy" or a
"fairy tale," it was not until the period of the Enlightenment in the
eighteenth century, or, for Eastern European Jews, the burgeoning of
the Haskalah, or rational movement, in the nineteenth century, that
such rubrics were used. To do so helped to distinguish the imaginative from the real. In medieval times, demons or helping spirits were
considered to be living and functional entities who entered the
earthly sphere to work in favor or to the detriment of humankind.
The Bible, the Talmud, and commentaries upon them, as well as
other religious texts—considered the foundations of a code of laws
and way of life—referred to fantastic animals as implicit in the
religious conventions of the day. The rationalists of the Haskalah
movement—a process similar to the one that had already begun
taking effect in Christian circles—rejected the irrational and mystical traditions in Judaism.

Both mystical and critical approaches seem fitting in our explication of "The Rabbi Who Was Turned into a Werewolf." A ration-
ally oriented study using differentiation and evaluation to point up
archetypal behavioral patterns in the tale may help us understand

the forces at stake in medieval times—which have been carried over into today's world. Both conscious and subliminal domains come into play in elaboration of this enigmatic and provocative work, whether it is viewed as a product of the religious experience or simply taken at face value.

The powerful conflictual motivations and personality distortions plaguing the Jewish community during medieval times, as evidenced in the werewolf tale, encourage multiple interpretations. For some, the tale is pure fantasy, disclosing no rapport with historical conditions. For others, this story of an evil wife trying to dominate her altruistic rabbi husband is a paradigm of a misogynist cultural condition existing within the Jewish community and also throughout Europe at the time. That certain associations may be made between the medieval tale and the highly complex and enigmatic biblical legend of Balaam (Numbers 22:24) adds another dimension to the discourse, universalizing as well as eternalizing its scope and impact even on sophisticated contemporary audiences.

What were the significant events in the Balaam tale that the medieval mind found so pertinent? Balaam, a heathen prophet, was requested by Balak, the king of Moab, to curse the Israelites. The Hebrews—who, following their Exodus from Egypt and their forty-year stay in the wilderness were en route to Canaan, as the biblical tale suggests—represented a threat to the ruling tribal kings. Because Balaam had experienced a visitation from God, instead of acquiescing to Balak's request he uttered a blessing on the Israelites. During the happenings—and this was, seemingly, the most popular part of the tale—Balaam's donkey began to talk: "How godly are thy tents O Jacob, and thy tabernacles, O Israel" (24:5). The esoteric meaning of the animal's ultrasignificant statement (it was uttered by Jews daily as they entered the synagogue to pray) has been debated for centuries by literalists and allegoricists.

What serves to increase the fascination of this biblical tale is its ambiguity. In keeping with Talmudic tradition, Balaam is regarded as a prophet on a par with Moses, even though in the biblical story he is portrayed as a purveyor of wickedness: it was on his advice that the Midianites lured Israel to immorality and idolatry. Nevertheless, it is argued that because God spoke through the mouth of the heathen Balaam, Judaism's message is both universal and eternal. Moreover, that the donkey spoke God's words also suggested the importance of the animal world in the learning experience that is life. As indicated in the fable, spirit (humankind), working in consort with the instinctual (animal) realm rather than in opposition to this power, imparts wisdom—unfathomable mysteries.

"The Rabbi Who Was Turned into a Werewolf" invites readers to penetrate the closed society of a deeply religious man who has spent his life and whatever money is at his disposal in performing good works for the poor and has also inculcated in his students the highest values his faith and life have to offer. His wife, however, is not of the same ilk. Shrewd, materialistic, and power hungry, she is interested mainly in jewels, clothes, and other adornments. Suddenly, and for no apparent reason, the rabbi loses his money, and rather than face the pain of not being able to fund his charitable works, he leaves town along with fifty students. It is during his exoteric journey that he comes upon a magic ring that grants him any and all wishes. He asks for and is given enough gold to return with his students to his town, where he continues distributing the necessities of life to the needy.

So as not to get ahead of ourselves, the rest of the tale—including the rabbi's transformation into a werewolf and his wife's into a donkey—will not be revealed until later in the course of our analysis. However, we may already suggest that the supernatural events dramatized—the first of which relates to the magic ring—indicate in part a struggle waged within the rabbi's personal psychology: seemingly unregenerate or archaic shadow forces are at work as he attempts to pursue his altruistic desires while also coping with his demanding wife/anima. Or the tale could also be viewed as the story of a neglected wife, whose enraged animus reaches violent proportions. That characters are transformed from their human condition to animal forms—as was common practice in literary works since ancient and classical times: Aesop, Apuleius, Ovid, La Fontaine—enriches the range of our medieval Jewish tale. In many cases animals, emerging as they do from subliminal regions, may be either destructive or productive. In either case, they are frequently, but not always, helpful to individuals in understanding problematic conditions that might otherwise have gone unnoticed and unrectified.

The Altruistic Rabbi as Wanderer

Wanderings or journeys in fairy tales, myths, or homiletic narratives (Odysseus, Parzival, Aeneas, Dante) may be viewed as paradigms of initiation rituals, as quests for greater knowledge or concerted searches for one's spiritual and psychological center: the Divine (Self) in each individual. They entail, most habitually, a series of obstacles set in the hero's path, which he must evaluate and analytically separate into their constituent elements, thereby enlightening himself as to his future course.

In our medieval story, all has seemingly been going well for the rabbi. The same is true for Balaam in the biblical tale. Both men enjoy fine reputations. Having earned the respect of the individual groups they serve, they have also succeeded in indulging their need for adulation. Why, then, has this enjoyable and productive period suddenly vanished in both their cases? They have evidently reached an impasse—or, as Jung suggested, have become "stuck" in their psychological and spiritual evolution—as sometimes happens when "the resources of the conscious mind are exhausted" (Jung 1966, par. 84). If, generally speaking, the status quo is maintained for too long a period, decay is likely to set in. The rabbi and Balaam, it may be suggested, each in his own way has reached a crossroad. At this point, choices have to be made so as to be able to carve out new paths.

Let us first explore the rabbi's situation. His wandering or archetypal journey through time and space, accompanied by his fifty students, is not to be viewed as a desire to escape from an unpleasant condition but rather as a rite of passage. The journeying or traveling process gives an individual or group the possibility of facing and coping with a variety of difficulties. Hadn't the Jews, who spent forty years in the desert during their Exodus, learned to function under extreme duress? To be alone, isolated from one's community and from the support it could give individuals and groups, obliges people to use whatever ingenuity they have at their disposal in order to survive. It also teaches a person to dig deeply into his own subliminal spheres, as Odysseus, Orpheus, and Aeneas, among others, had done, thus encountering new vistas that altered what might be termed their peacefully stagnant attitudes.

The rabbi in our tale, like a priest, doctor, shaman, or prophet, is an archetypal father figure: a psychopomp. A positive, nourishing, and conscious force, he represents order as opposed to instinctive, spontaneous, or unconscious pulsions that might topple the cultural arrangement that works so well for the society of which he is a part. A potential figure of transcendence, the rabbi symbolizes a timeless and divinely inspired being, able to help establish earthly wisdom and justice. Culturally, he stands for what is and what could be. Even he, however, who is the worker of good deeds and the spiritual leader of a community, has come to terms neither with his shadow (defined as an unconscious part of one's personality containing those elements the ego considers negative or unacceptable and would like to annihilate) nor with his anima (the unconscious feminine aspect of a man's personality). His overly one-sided existence, although benefiting the collective, is evidently insufficient in the personal domain.

A deeper drama is being played out behind the rabbi's seeming godliness and his sudden financial divestiture, which he, understandably, attributes to Divine will. Never, however, does he question his motivations for being so assiduously preoccupied with benevolence and with teaching. We may well ask whether there might not be, on an unconscious level, a kind of egotistical intent involved. Indeed, charity is one of the most laudable ways of earning the admiration of many. Isn't the rabbi's munificence, therefore, an infallible way of enhancing his prestige vis-á-vis the community? Rather than probing the various factors that compel him to indulge in his charitable mission while also exploring his inability to face his sudden loss of fortune—an inability that prevents him from openly sharing his divestiture with his people—he decides to spare himself the certain humiliation of his turn of fortune and to leave the community. To save face, then, is instrumental in his decision to keep his poverty a secret. As of necessity, he informs his wife of his economic downfall, as he does the fifty students who will share his exile.

His new life of wanderings and hardships could be instrumental, as it was in Odysseus's case among others, in increasing his consciousness concerning his own inner promptings. For example, what actually lies behind his persona (social face) that he is so intent upon preserving intact? To effect a transformation within the rabbi's psyche, however, would require a disordering of his former position as spiritual leader of his community—even, perhaps, a loss of his equilibrium. A *tabula rasa*, in essence, must be effected to make it possible for him to *know* a different lifestyle and, as such, to make new connections.

To look into those factors that our rabbi shares with the biblical Balaam may allow us to better understand their affinity and the impact these two archetypal tales have on readers. As the story is recounted in Numbers, Balaam had reached the zenith of his power: as prophet (his prediction that Balak would wear the royal crown having been fulfilled) and also as sorcerer and interpreter of dreams. Although Balak was an even greater magician and sooth-sayer than Balaam, there was one part of the future that he had envisioned that he did not understand. He had already foreseen that he would be the cause of the death of twenty-four thousand Israelites, but he did not know how this event was to come to pass. Furthermore, he was not satisfied with partial elimination; he wanted to destroy all of them. To this end, as previously mentioned, he asked Balaam to curse Israel, thus hoping to prevent the Hebrews from entering the Holy Land. Agreeing at first to Balak's request, Balaam refused to comply with his petition after the ''spirit of God came upon him.'' Three times Balak sent messengers to the prophet hoping to change his mind. Three times Balaam told him he would not comply, offering different excuses each time. Apparently, Balaam finally admitted the truth of the interdict—God said, ''Thou shalt not curse the people of Israel: for they are blessed'' (Numbers 22:12)—but not its binding force.

In like manner did the rabbi of our medieval tale refrain from uttering the truth to his community concerning his economic divesture. Equally arresting is the fact that the rabbi lived in Uz (Hebrew, ''fertile land''), seemingly in Bohemia, a town bearing the same name as the one in which the ''perfect and upright'' Job had made his home (Job 1:1). Does such an identification indicate that the rabbi, like Job, would also be put to the test, thereby setting the stage for the drama to be enacted?

Like Balaam, the rabbi was highly intelligent: he spoke seventy languages. He was adulated by the community not only because of his good works toward the needy and his strong interest in further-ing the education of poor students at the yeshivah, but because of his belief in an egalitarian society: his home was open to all who were hungry. His wife, whose ideals were at odds with his, resented the presence of the poor in her home and the rabbi's continuous largesse and was hurt, as well, by his lack of attention and love. The uncon-scious slight she suffered catalyzed latent materialistic, aggressive, and destructive behavioral patterns into action.

Rather than questioning himself as to the nature of the sin he believed he had committed which resulted in his sudden penury and refusing to face inwardly feelings of humiliation and degradation (or to complain to others about his ill luck, since some in his commu-nity would certainly gloat over his sorrow), the rabbi took the outer and not the inner course for his hoped-for salvation. Similarly, Balaam's refusal to reveal the full force of God's interdict to curse Israel remained a mystery. In choosing such a course, Balaam was in fact falsifying God's message in three different ways, and each time he did so, he disclosed insights into his character. The first time that he rejected Balak's orders, he told the king's ambassadors—without mentioning God's name—that to appear in their company would be considered beneath his dignity. Thus he demonstrated arrogance and elitism. In his second statement, although he admitted that he would not go against God's injunction not to curse the people of Israel since they were "blessed," he claimed to have free will: he had the power to do as he liked but chose not to transgress the Divine interdict. That Balaam even thought of associating gold and silver with God's command in his third refusal reveals a fundamentally acquisitive nature: "Balak would give me his house full of silver and gold, I cannot go beyond the word of the Lord my God, to do less or more" (Numbers 22:18). Balaam's statement may also refer to the notion that no matter what his master offered, he could not possibly compensate him for his efforts. In all three instances, he was living out a conflictual and frustrated situation. Fundamentally, he wanted to carry out Balak's order, his jealousy of Israel's good fortune overriding any sense of integrity on his part.

Both Balaam and the rabbi, then, reveal a sense of shame and embarrassment at the thought of removing their persona. Neither is willing to speak the truth: the former is fearful of Balak's scorn and anger and his own loss of prestige, the latter unwilling to cope with the jeers and recriminations his poverty might bring to him. Both men are not only fundamentally greedy and envious, but their haughtiness prevents them from seeing clearly into the truth of their own smudged psyches. Balaam and the rabbi are unable to face a world in which—as they see it—their reputations will be sullied and their power principles diminished. The rabbi's gifts, although generous, have served to a great extent to enhance his prominence in the community. Were the truth to be known about his loss of fortune, and were Balaam to admit the full force of God's interdict, each would lose his illustrious reputation.

The unfortunate inner images the rabbi and Balaam bear of themselves are translated into haughtiness and vanity in the workaday world. Rather than considering their setbacks as implicit in the life process, each man, in his own way, reveals a weakly structured ego (center of consciousness), accounting for an inability to stand what they believe to be a humiliation. A loss of prestige, were the truth to be known, would in their eyes prevent them from maintaining an unsullied and distinguished persona: their unconscious goal.

More parallels may be made between Balaam and the rabbi. For example, for reasons of status, neither man begins his wanderings or journeys alone. Balaam is accompanied by two servants when he sets out to visit the princes of Moab. The rabbi takes fifty yeshivah students with him during his self-imposed exile. Before setting out he says to them: "I hope you will do toward me as I have always done toward you." Lauding their spiritual guide, they depart with high hopes of being worthy of God's love.

The Weasel and the Gold Ring

In the next step of the rabbi's initiatory travels, the similarities between his story and Balaam's cease, but there will be additional parallels further along.

After two years of roaming in search of redemption, the rabbi's meager funds run out. His entourage has no food or clothes and is reduced to begging. Isn't the rabbi now put in the position of the poor he has tried to help in his community? He, the great giver, must now be the seeker of charity. Another blow will befall the rabbi and his group. Rather than meeting with kindness each time they ask for food, doors are shut in their faces. Worn in heart and soul, the students finally ask the rabbi to let them return home to their parents. Yes, he replies, but enjoins them to wait until after the Sabbath—only another four or five days. They agree.

Upon reaching the countryside, the rabbi comes upon a clump of saplings. He tells the students to go ahead because he has to relieve himself. After doing so, he walks to a nearby spring where he washes his hands; then he continues on. Suddenly he sees a weasel run by "with a lovely gold ring in its mouth." He chases it a bit; the animal drops the ring; the rabbi picks it up. Although he realizes that the ring is worthless insofar as its gold content is concerned, an inscription on the inside of the ring catches his attention: "Though I look ugly, I am invaluable." Rooted to the spot, he realizes that something extraordinary has happened. "Perhaps it has the magic power to grant any wish that a man might desire," he says to himself. He decides to try: "May God let me find a money belt before me." Moments later, he sees a belt filled with gold lying before him.

Wise enough not to divulge the secret of the ring to his students, he is aware that without the maturity and wisdom necessary, such powers as he now possesses might fall into evil hands, bringing havoc rather than harmony. In addition, he is probably motivated by an unconscious wish not to share his power or money with anyone else. He tells the students that he is certain he will meet a rich man in the next town who will buy them new clothes and send them home. Predictably, that is what occurs.

What has the rabbi learned from his years of wandering and from the miracle of the weasel? Has he discovered the sin for which he believes God has punished him? If we are to consider God psychologically, as the Self (total psyche), we would suggest that the rabbi has been and still is blind to his own promptings. He certainly has no notion as to his motivations: the extent of his arrogance, which may have accounted, at least in part, for his blindness as to the role he formerly played as benevolent despot in his community. That he was lavish with his funds, lavish with his time, and lavish with his kindness was rewarded by the adulation of the poor. That he could not face a change of lifestyle from wealth to poverty indicated his ego's inability to descend from its exalted position as the community's leader. Although his actions in favor of the unfortunate were commendable, charity, as has already been suggested, is a double-edged sword: what others take to be generosity and compassion may also nourish a need in the giver for glorification and sanctification. We may add that such a dynamic may also feed the giver's unconscious feelings of inadequacy or guilt, of fundamental subservience or inferiority.

Like a ruler bogged down in his own daily routine, the rabbi as dispenser of charity had followed all the rituals expected of him to the letter. Because he had not probed the symbolic meanings of the spiritual disciplines he practiced nor explored the motivations of his actions, he had not, psychologically speaking, come into contact with that living collective power within him—Deity (Self). His psychic potential, therefore, remained unfulfilled.

Despite the sense of degradation he suffered when begging, he had not even begun to explore his inner paucity. Nevertheless, some positive transformation had been effected. Change had taken place not via rational or spiritual means, but, surprisingly, as a result of bodily needs. Viscera took precedence over spirit; the empirical, not the celestial, realm cried out its wants. The rabbi's sense of cleanliness, which is implicit in Jewish religious dicta (rabbis and holy men are required to wash their hands several times during the religious services in the synagogue, thus paralleling the ritual of continuous spiritual purification), motivated him to find the spring. It was following his ablutions that he spied the weasel, after which the extraterrestrial event ensued.

What did these various steps in the transformation ritual indicate? Excrement in some cultures symbolizes a sacred biological power residing in human beings which, when evacuated, as in dung, may lead to fruitfulness. In some African cultures, such as the Libouka of the Congo and the Fali in the northern part of Cameroon, special rites are effected around human dejecta, since, it is believed, everything emerging from the visceral region has "mana-charge" and is therefore sacred. Semen, urine, dung, flatus, and other bodily excretions are all believed to be creative powers. Indeed, the highest class of initiates among the Bambaras of Mali practice ritual coprophagy. In the Aztec pantheon, the name of the goddess of physical love and fecundity, Tlazolteotl, means "eater of garbage" or "goddess of filth" (Neumann 1954, p. 25).

The dichotomy existing between some African religious traditions with regard to the notion of dejecta and the views of Westerners concerning excrement is vast. What the latter believe to be devoid of value, impure, and discharge as a noxious bodily function, the former consider beneficial. To use alchemical parlance, it is considered as great as gold. Although far from acceding to such beliefs, the rabbi, unconsciously, acts according to these convictions. His hand-washing ritual, unbeknown to him, has instituted a whole mysterious process of transformation.

Since water originates and therefore begins its trajectory beneath the earth, everything it contains is unformed, in a state of virtuality, *in potentia*. Thus water is considered the source of life and rebirth. In Jeremiah we read of water's crucial significance: "For my people have committed two evils; they have forsaken me the fountain of living waters, and hewed them out cisterns, broken cisterns, that can hold no water" (2:13). In keeping with the notion of water as *prima materia*, the ablutions performed by the rabbi indicate a symbolic return to the *source* of everything. Furthermore, this symbolism points the way to his possible rebirth via some future regressive act on his part to an archaic stage in his evolution. In Proverbs we are told that wisdom emerges from water:

"The words of a man's mouth are as deep waters, and the wellspring of wisdom as a flowing brook" (18:4). Again: "Counsel in the heart of man is like deep water, but a man of understanding will draw it out" (20:5).

Spring water, like holy water, is pure in essence, emerging as it does from the depths of Mother Earth; and in the form of rain it falls from the heights of heaven, quenching the ground's thirst. The combination of liquids descending from celestial regions and those emerging from the depths of Mother Earth is viewed as archetypal because of their universality and eternality. Their fusion in our story becomes the source of the rabbi's evolution. By washing his hands he has immersed them not in Plato's sacred Lethe (waters of forgetfulness) but in those of recollection (or memory). Because an individual's inner life and spiritual energy originates from these waters, Jung associated them with the unconscious. To return to the past via remembrance, be it on an empirical or archetypal level, suggests that memory is considered to be no longer a mere receptacle but an active participant in furthering an individual's sacred initiatory journey. Psychologically viewed, the melding of terrestrial and celestial spheres, earth and sky, or time and timelessness, yields gnosis.

In that spring water is never still but always active, it, like the collective unconscious, prevents visibility into its depths. Only via indirection or intuition can conclusions—and these at best are only temporary—be drawn (von Franz 1988, 183–5). The question remains as to whether the rabbi will be able to see his shadow when peering into mobile waters. Would his doppelgänger (a living being's ghostly or spiritual double) become visible?

The rabbi's powers of mentation have, nevertheless, developed, since he not only did not discard the monetarily worthless ring but took seriously the message inscribed inside: "Though I look ugly, I am invaluable." Insight, then, has led him to realize the deeper implications involved: inner rather than exterior developments have proven to be of great significance in the life experience.

Why did an animal and not a mysterious human being appear on the scene to enlighten the rabbi? Animals in fairy tales, myths, and legends are frequently archetypal in nature, representing inner faults or deficiencies in the unconscious/conscious dynamic of the person projecting onto them. What was lacking in the rabbi's case was an understanding of the motivations for his acts—whether in terms of intimate human relationships, particularly with his wife, or of spiritual relationships with the community he led. Nor had he any inkling of how best to plan for the future. In that animals are archetypal, they live outside of time or in a metatime, and thus are immortal. In this capacity, they are empowered to open doors to individuals unable to see beyond their own linearity. Hadn't Democritus (470–360 B.C.E.) suggested that animals might be viewed as mirror images of psychic movements: thoughts as well as affects? Whatever the animal, its presence under certain circumstances may work on the psyche for ill or for good (von Franz 1988, p. 38). Because the rabbi could not depend on his own resources to perform effectively (he failed to acquire funds and his students wanted to leave him), the animal archetype was drawn upon to compensate for his personal deficiencies (Jung, *CW* 9i, par. 398).

Why, above all other animals, had the weasel been chosen to further the rabbi's evolution? What factors does the weasel represent in the rabbi's personality? First, it is known as a cunning, agile, flesh-eating mammal. Second, it feeds on mice, rats, moles, and small birds and is useful in destroying vermin in barns and granaries. Because the weasel is clever in a worldly sense, its feet firmly planted on earth, it knows how to care for itself under difficult circumstances. Skillful, shrewd, crafty, deceitful, it relies only upon itself and its aggressive ways to sustain its life. The weasel, like the owl and the hare, is considered a negative feminine image, suggesting a cold, calculating, cunning, but also cruel manner (von Franz 1970, III:10). Such archetypal characteristics are associated with both the shadow and the anima. Since the rabbi is naive, artless, gullible, trusting, and repressed, the weasel possesses those qualities the rabbi lacks.

As a spiritual leader, the rabbi has until now leaned on his students and on the community at large to enhance his feelings of self-worth. His wanderings, unlike those of Odysseus, for example, have not helped him rid himself of those unregenerate contents existing within his subliminal sphere that impede spiritual and psychological fulfillment. The libido generated by the image of the weasel holding the gold ring in its mouth so charges his unconscious that rather than rushing back to his students, he is sidetracked and follows it. The law of compensation, becoming effective in the fusion of the images of the weasel and the gold ring, enables him to recognize what complementarity he needs to discover—that is, his own center.

That all that glitters is not gold is a truism in the rabbi's case. Yet it is the lure of what his imagination considers to be a valuable metal (although worthless in the collective domain) that brings him the verbal treasure, "Though I look ugly, I am invaluable," which he rapidly transforms into valuable matter. The circularity of rings, whether magic or not, symbolizes eternality, thus attachment, alliance, unification, wholeness, a bond existing between members of a community and between an individual and the Divinity. For Elada in the Irish Cu Chulainn cycle, the ring represented science; for Prometheus, the iron ring was associated with submission. In both cases, it stood for mystery. On an esoteric level, a magic ring—Solomon's ring, according to Arab myths—may reveal to the bearer that "invaluable" element he or she so covets, that is, the gold of wisdom with which it is equated. To acquire such a ring is to open a door onto another sphere of existence; to achieve greater understanding and knowledge of earthly and cosmic matters. Because rings in their roundness are also identified with time and space—infinity—they never begin nor do they end. As a wedding band made of non-precious metal, the rabbi's ring suggests the worthlessness of his marriage—or those elements representative of the feminine principle. Only the message inscribed on the inside of the ring, and whatever treasure it may yield, is of import to him.

That the rabbi decides not to reveal the secret of the ring but rather to preserve silence about its miraculous qualities—a condition that fosters miracles—indicates weasellike cunning. When he informs his students of the wealthy man they are to meet in the next town, he appears to have been endowed with an increased insight into human nature. Unlike Parzival, who failed to ask the right question at the right time, thus proving himself insufficiently evolved to become the knight of the Holy Grail, the rabbi does forge ahead in that he heeds the advice he sees incised in the ring and acts accordingly.

The Werewolf: The Negative Anima/Animus at Work

The fear, disorientation, and sense of bereavement suffered by the poor in his absence abates now that the rabbi has returned to his hometown. Their spiritual leader's behavioral pattern remains mostly unchanged. He resumes his charity work, providing food and shelter for the needy and instruction for the yeshivah students.

As already suggested, the rabbi's blindness to the motives behind his benevolent acts suggests pride as well as feelings of superiority vis-á-vis both the community and his wife. In that she is a living projection of the rabbi's anima, it may be suggested that her husband has become the embodiment of her animus (the unconscious masculine side of a woman's personality). Belittled and starved for affection throughout her married life, she naturally craves more and more love and tenderness from her neglectful husband. Because these qualities are in such meager supply, she has become an animus-driven woman. Her insatiable thirst for eros reaches demonlike proportions. The demands made by her animus are no different in negative potential than those any impoverished person would make on the well-to-do. Little by little, however, as her animus begins taking on increasing virulence, the rabbi's anima expands into a blind, negative, destructive force.

Because his wife knows the reason for the rabbi's departure from town, she understandably questions him upon his return about his newly acquired wealth. "Dear husband, how come you have so much money all at once? We were so poor earlier that you left town." Weasellike, the rabbi makes a guarded answer: "The Good Lord sent me some luck during my travels." Disbelieving, she plagues him with so many questions that he finally reveals to her the secret of the golden ring. Coveting the object that could bring her a fortune, she begins wondering what wiles she could use to acquire it. "I can see you don't love me anymore," she says. "Otherwise you wouldn't be afraid to trust me with the ring." Caught off guard, the rabbi sheds his newly acquired weasellike cunning, yields under the pressure, and gives her the ring. Seconds later, she puts her head under the covers and speaks as follows: "I wish that God would turn my husband into a werewolf and let him run around in the forest with the wild beasts." As soon as she says this, the rabbi leaps out of the window and dashes off into the deep forest, the Böhmerwald. From that day on, the wife is able to indulge her lust for gold and her greed for material possessions freely and unabashedly. Unlike her husband, however, she never distributes any alms nor allows the poor to enter her home.

As a werewolf, the narrative tells us, the rabbi is transformed into a destructive, devouring power. In the case of this type of parapsychological event, such a metamorphosis understandably arouses fear in the onlooker. It may trigger an attitude of curiosity and fascination as well (von Franz 1970, I:9). Both reactions are operational in the werewolf/rabbi situation. In keeping with his newly acquired animallike habits, he builds himself a dry den in the forest in which to live and, again according to instinct, mutilates and murders anyone coming near him: "he caused terrible suffering and tore apart people and other animals." No one is stronger than he; nor does anyone dare go near him, for he is more powerful than a lion and "as smart as a human being."

What is a werewolf, that the rabbi's wife would wish such a fate on her husband? In ancient and modern times, in bestiaries and in works of fiction, this imaginary animal represented a man temporarily or eternally transformed into a wolf. In cases of lycanthropy, otherwise known as delirium of metamorphosis, an individual believed himself to have acquired the same characteristics as the wolf—most appropriately his supposed appetite for human flesh (although modern research has shown that wolves aren't usually a threat to humans). Many variations of the werewolf myth exist depending on the centuries and the regions. In the *Satyricon* of Petronius (d.66 C.E.), for example, Niceros's guide turns into a werewolf. In his *Historia Naturalis*, Pliny (23–79 C.E.) indicated that the Arcadian mountains were filled with werewolves. During the medieval period and Renaissance, legends of werewolves abounded in Europe. In 1573, for example, Gilles Garnier, living in Dole, France, was declared guilty after having confessed to committing werewolf crimes and was burned at the stake. One of the most popular werewolf stories is the ever-terrifying *Dracula* by Bram Stoker (1897), whose protagonist is a man by day and a wolf by night. Even in 1925, cases of lycanthropy were reported as having occurred in Alsace (Summers 1973, pp. 23–4, 448).

Real or imaginary animals appear frequently in myths. In the *Odyssey*, for example, Athena reveals herself (although not in animal form) only to Odysseus and to the dogs of the swineherd Eumaeus, not to Telemachus, who remains blind to her reality; Pausanius wrote that at Olympia, racehorses saw the ghost of a former hero and shied at the spot where he was buried (Gaster 1969, p. 309). The werewolf, like the weasel of our story, is archetypal in nature. Because such images appear in the collective, or historical, psyche of the people of the time, they are invested with great affectivity. Primitive individuals do not differentiate contents of the collective psyche from those of the individual consciousness, believing them to be "self-evident realities" (Jung 1970, par. 150). Because of the unconscious nature of the werewolf archetype in our story, it may be viewed as a double projection: that of the wife's animus as well as of the rabbi's shadow.

Projection implies an act of thrusting or throwing forward—"a process whereby an unconscious quality or content of one's own is perceived and reacted to in an outer object" (Edinger 1978, pp. 147–50). Although on a realistic level one finds the transformation of a man into a werewolf incredible, one might suggest that just as electrical waves are invisible to the naked eye (despite the fact that they exist as both psychological and physical forces), they are made manifest in such equipment as television (Harding 1975, p. 44). In this connection, didn't Tertullian (160–230 c.e.) state about his Christian faith: "It is certain because it is impossible"? The mind, under certain circumstances, has a way of turning fantasy and even the grotesque into reality.

To project, then, is to attribute or assign to others characteristics that we love or hate. While we believe that the qualities we ascribe to an individual or to a group belong to others, they are, in fact, our own. We are unaware of their presence within us, since they exist inchoate in our subliminal sphere. To be used in a positive manner, however, they need conscious development, after which they must be integrated into the psyche. To be obsessed unconsciously with a projection, as in the case of the wife's animus possession, is to be caught in it. Only by becoming aware of this kind of archaic and primitive content within her unconscious can she begin to come to terms with it. Since no confrontation with her animus has occurred, the projection took on life the minute the rabbi/werewolf leaped out of the window and ran into the forest to live.

That an animal as voracious and bloodthirsty as the werewolf has been intertwined into the happenings in no way devalues the rabbi's formerly positive performance in the community. It merely points to the fact that until the blindness of his self-willed ego begins to see and do battle with an unbridled inner power (his shadow), it cannot bring what his wife views as a destructive force into consciousness. Indeed, under such circumstances, we might say that his ego has, at least temporarily, been displaced as the center of his personality (Harding 1975, p. 67). The rabbi has not only felt threatened by the mysteries of the dark side of the feminine principle he experienced, he has compensated for his terror of the chthonic, or irrational, sphere by experiencing it in himself. That havoc ensues, then, is understandable. As Jung wrote: "Wisdom seeks the middle path and pays for this audacity by a dubious affinity with daemon and beast, and so is open to moral misinterpretation" (Jung, CW 9i, par. 420).

The forest to which the werewolf goes—analogous to the domain of the unconscious, where the terror of one's own revelations brings on panic attacks—is the perfect habitat for it to live out its unregenerate instinctuality. The forest for the Greeks (*Dodona*), the French (*Broceliande*), the Hindus (*Dandaka*), and others, was considered the sanctuary of the Great Mother. It is amid this immensely fertile area that she rules over vegetative and animal life and that she fulfills her existence as perpetual genetrix. Continuously transforming with regard to color, scent, shape, and consistency, she represents the mysterious process of growth that begins within the earth and is brought to term by means of water. Under her protection lives a lawless and confused world that, depending upon the circumstances, may bring death or salvation (the Great Mother in her voracious or her milk-giving aspects) (Neumann 1963, p. 51).

The dialectics involved in the relationship between anima and animus are difficult to sort out. For the rabbi's wife to function as powerfully as she has done indicates a fundamental weakness in her husband's rapport with her. His emotional detachment, aloofness, or *apatheia* toward his mate—paralleling that of Socrates toward Xanthippe—has caused an overly emotional condition to develop in the rabbi's wife. For her, the rabbi takes on reality under the guise of a vicious despoiler. Like Socrates, the rabbi's buildup of a superior consciousness has cut him off from his archaic animal involvement, and hence he has rejected his anima and the feminine aspect of eros which, under proper circumstances, could have worked in his favor (von Franz 1970, II:8). The rabbi's wife takes revenge on an emotionally unsatisfactory situation by projecting onto her husband the lethal image of the werewolf, which, at least in her mind, points to the subordinate position he now plays in their partnership. A parallelism and rhythmic interchange is effected in the unconscious projections of both husband and wife: the greater her feelings of rejection and frustration, the angrier she grows and the crueler are the actions of her animus, the wild and domineering beast within her. Although her husband is the one to be transformed into the werewolf, he is, as of necessity, living out her animus.

After the rabbi's metamorphosis into a werewolf, his ego becomes so identified with its instinctive components that it assumes the directorship of his aggressive and destructive acts. Yet it could be said that because he is now behaving like the animal, he is in harmony with his instinctual world. However, he is also deviating from a human being's rational and conscious ends, so he is not properly integrated. His instinctual nature is actuating his entire frame of being during his werewolf period; he is connected neither with consciousness nor with the spiritual domain. His forest life is dominated by the Earth Mother, whose prey he really is. Since she holds him captive, his world revolves around a moist, dark, and elemental domain (Neumann 1954, p. 308). The rabbi/werewolf's choice of the forest in which to live out his unbridled and savage acts confirms a need to come to terms with his anima as well as to explore his shadow world. Only then will the unconscious pulsations surging within him—and urging him on to dismember any and all human beings who venture too near—cease to operate.

A plethora of such devouring individuals and/or cultural antinomies have become the subject of literary masterpieces throughout the centuries. In the *Bacchae* (408–406 B.C.E.), for example, Euripides gave audiences an unforgettable dramatization of the ego's desire to eradicate rather than to explicate, to condemn and destroy instead of integrating negative components inhabiting the psyche. When Agave, King Pentheus's mother, and her followers, the Bacchants, indulge in their *sparagmos* (dismemberment) ritual and *omophagia* (eating of human flesh) ceremony, unknowingly killing her son, they are symbolically taking the first step in an attempt to fragment, thus transform, a negative collective attitude toward woman in Greece. It was Euripides' way of bringing an overly patriarchal cultural dilemma—a faulty ruling principle—into the open.

Agave, a *vagina dentata* type, "devours" her son. Although the rabbi's wife does not cause her husband's death by transforming him into a werewolf, she erroneously believes that she has gotten rid of an eros-less force in the household. Nothing is further from the truth. She has failed to annihilate what she considers to be her husband's intransigent and destructive characteristics: his lack of understanding of her emotional needs. After his departure, she remains the same. What is different, however, is her newfound freedom, which allows her to give vent to her acquisitiveness, thereby filling the giant maw in her affectionless life with worldly things (Neumann 1954, pp. 351–2).

Like Agave, the rabbi's wife is the victim of extremes and irrationality, acting and reacting to given situations impulsively. Unbeknownst to the psychologically unevolved rabbi, she has for years been tearing his male psyche to pieces, pulling and tugging at it with her rapacious, vindictive, and demonic ways. Her frustrations reach such volcanic magnitude as to transform her libido into a living and functioning werewolf (Neumann 1963, p. 307). As the rabbi's belittled and unattended anima, she has lived in a shadowy world rooted in the subsoil of his unconscious, the deepest abyss within the personality (Neumann 1954, p. 353). Both realistically and psychologically, it could be said that she has been "the guardian of the threshold," that is, of the rabbi's house and psyche. Is it any wonder that an irresolvable conflict has existed between ego and shadow in an anima/animus dynamic?

Not only is the rabbi unable to relate to his anima, but this feminine component is imprisoned in the body of a werewolf. Living in a circumscribed forest habitat, he exists, as previously mentioned, as a split-off complex: as "otherness," as instinctual nature only. In no way does the werewolf resemble any of the rabbi's positive attributes. Were his anima to be released from the stranglehold of his unconscious, it might have a chance of eventually becoming integrated into his personality. If such were possible, he might begin to relate to the feminine principle on a conscious level, thereby transforming it (his wife) into a valuable part of the whole.

The Fearless Hero

The townspeople have become so fearful of the werewolf that they ask the "charcoal-burners" to try to destroy him. Because the werewolf is "stronger than a lion and as smart as a human being," the charcoal-burners dare not comply. Apprised of the increasingly dangerous situation, the king sets out to trap the creature himself but fails in his mission. He then proclaims that whoever captures the werewolf will not only be given his beautiful daughter in marriage, but his kingdom as well. His advisor, a young hero who has fought in many wars, undertakes the task.

Meanwhile, despite the werewolf's vicious nature, there is one particular charcoal-burner living in the forest whom he has not tried to kill and who has never been harmed by the animal. In fact, the werewolf likes the charcoal-burner so much that he is forever hanging around his hut. Such a situation is not surprising in view of the fact that the werewolf/rabbi, as a living projection of his wife's animus, responds well to kindness, or at least a nonhostile attitude, on the part of a male. Indeed, the animal reacts spontaneously and emotionally to the attention his own wife has craved.

In terms of the werewolf/rabbi's personality, however, the charcoal-burner may be viewed as an understanding and wise shadow figure with whom he seeks companionship. Since he cannot convey his need for humankind via word but only in deed, he lives out his forest existence in a state of submission to a fundamental disparity within his nature: destructive in that he kills people and constructive in his friendship with the charcoal-burner.

When the hero sets out to conquer the werewolf—as Theseus slew the minotaur in the depths of the Cretan labyrinth, Siegfried his dragon in the Teutonic forest, and Beowolf the monster Grendel, who lived with his mother in a murky pond—he seeks to rid the world of a destructive, regressive collective power. Ordered in his thought processes, the hero first seeks out the charcoal-burner who has befriended the animal in the forest, informing him that he intends to kill it. He is told, however, that "when the wolf sees you, you will be doomed no matter how great you are." Fearless, as are most inexperienced heroes, the inflated young man refuses to listen to the charcoal-burner's wise counsel. Instead, he takes it upon himself to destroy what no one else has been able to destroy. Impatiently he says: "Don't hold me up! This is what has to be!" To this the charcoal-burner replies: "God have mercy on your soul!" Unable to dissuade the hero, the charcoal-burner leads him to the animal's lair. Although the hero is armed with musket and spear, the werewolf/rabbi flings him to the ground. As he is about to kill him, the charcoal-burner intervenes and chases the animal away. Rather than learning his lesson, the hero refuses to lay down his arms. Three times he tries to kill the animal, who becomes increasingly fierce after each attempt. Only when he is finally aware of the reality of his plight does the hero plead with God to save him from the wolf. He swears to his God that he wouldn't go after him anymore, and the animal responds by wagging its tail.

Fear, having triggered faith in the hero, accounts for the change in the course of his action. Rather than focusing on the instant gratification of his immature ego, that is, on the killing factor, his prayer to God is an appeal to the Self (the entire psyche). Thus the hero has been able to put things into perspective and, in so doing, to start acquiring wisdom and understanding. No longer brash and aggressive in his attitude, he reacts, as had the charcoal-burner, to the animal's need for affection. Like a dog who had bared his teeth only as long as it was necessary to protect himself from danger, the werewolf/rabbi, now that he is no longer to be hunted, shows his appreciation and happiness by befriending the hero. When the hero turns to leave the forest, basically still fearing the animal, the werewolf/rabbi runs after him. So persistent is his need for a show of kindness that the hero finally removes his belt and uses it as a leash for the animal. Not only do the two become steady companions, but the animal henceforth acts as the hero's protector.

Why the change in the werewolf/rabbi? If we consider the animal as a hunted, maligned, and rejected shadow force, we can see that once he is accepted for what he is and treated with understanding, his viciousness abates. As animus, moreover, he responds to a show of feeling and relatedness. Having lived out his shadow side in a forest habitat and having gained the friendship of both the charcoal-burner and the hero, he now seeks to integrate these newly acquired "human"—in the best sense of the word—components into his personality.

Similarly, the hero has been transformed during his terrifying ordeal. No longer will he succumb to the temptation of overt and ego-dominated heroism, nor will he seek the shortest route to reach his goal, thus risking being overcome or devoured by the abysmal monster inhabiting his depths. The wisest of ways to approach his goal has become operational: calling upon Divinity, the Self, for healing. In so doing, he has opened himself up to the collective psyche, and therefore to the possibility of renewal. To kill the monster so as to earn individual glory and happiness is no longer his goal. His communication with Divinity (Self) reveals a belief in something higher: he has become less intransigent, having learned the meaning of friendship and spiritual commitment. His increasing maturity has now made him worthy of marrying the king's daughter and of eventually ruling her father's kingdom.

It is at this juncture that we return to the biblical Balaam, whose name in Hebrew means "Devourer of Nations" and who had comported himself in a similar manner to the rabbinical werewolf. When, in his younger days, Balaam had been in Egypt, it was he who had counseled the pharaoh to force the enslaved Israelites to make bricks. Were he again to yield to his avaricious and ego-dominated nature and curse Israel as Balak had requested of him, he would have, like Agave, indulged in the *sparagmos* ritual: instrumental in "tearing apart" a whole people limb from limb. Instead, however, God (Self) intervened, forbidding his voracious (werewolf) desires to be his guide.

How did God teach Balaam his lesson? Despite the fact that God had allowed him to set out with the princes of Moab, He peered into Balaam's heart and saw wickedness. Unaware of the insight, Balaam started out on his donkey, as was his habit, to reach his destination. (Balaam's donkey had been given to him by Jacob, who hoped that upon his arrival in Egypt he would advise the pharaoh not to harm the Israelites.) However, before Balaam arrived at the city of his host, "the angel of the Lord stood in a path of the vineyards" (Numbers 22:25). This angel was visible to the donkey, although not to Balaam, so the animal "turned aside out of the way" of the angel and went into the field. So outraged was Balaam by his inability to control the donkey's apparently obstreperous action (which was especially humiliating because it was witnessed by those accompanying him) that he smote the animal. When for the second time the angel of the Lord appeared to the donkey, "she thrust herself unto the wall" and in so doing crushed her master's foot, whereupon he smote her once again. The third time the angel of the Lord appeared to the donkey, she lay down and refused to move from the spot. Balaam dealt her a third blow with his staff.

Only at this point did the Lord open the donkey's mouth and allow her to speak, a gift that the animal had had since the sixth day of Creation, according to biblical exegesis, but had never been allowed to use until now. "What have I done unto thee, that thou hast smitten me those three times?" the animal asked (22:28). Balaam replied: "Because thou hast mocked me: I would there were a sword in mine hand, for now would I kill thee" (22:29). The animal then replied: "Am not I thine ass, upon which thou hast ridden ever since I was thine unto this day? Was I ever wont to do so unto thee?" (22:30). These words revealed the futility of Balaam's actions and the uselessness of his wicked imprecations against Israel. Only now did the Lord, in a spiritual sense, open Balaam's eyes:

. . . and he saw the angel of the Lord standing in the way, and his sword drawn in his hand: and he bowed down his head, and fell flat on his face. And the angel of the Lord said unto him, Wherefore hast thou smitten thine ass these three times? Behold, I went out to withstand thee, because thy way is perverse before me. (Numbers 22:31–32)

Balam admitted his evil acts:

. . . I have sinned; for I knew not that thou stoodest in the way against me: now therefore, if it displease thee, I will get me back again. (22:34)

Why does the number three appear here, as it does in the earlier part of the Balaam myth when Balak had requested that Balaam curse Israel? For mystics, the number three not only brings synthesis to thesis and antithesis, but it is considered the number of manifestation. Both Balaam and the hero in "The Rabbi Who Was Turned into a Werewolf" are given sight (intuition, wisdom) after three violent and unsuccessful attempts to reach their goal. Their inability to save face and the limited range of vision of each man's ego yield to the power of Divinity or Self, thus broadening their understanding of the forces at stake. That the donkey is awarded the power of speech in Balaam's case is intended as a warning to him to beware of the power of words issuing from his mouth and to refrain from cursing Israel.

Just as the ass saved Balaam's life by leading him out of the way of the angel of the Lord, whose sword was drawn to punish him for his "perverse" ways, so the charcoal-burner attempted to intervene in the werewolf/rabbi's fight with the hero by pointing out the inequity of the battle. Although he failed to change the hero's mind, a larger power, Divinity, took matters in hand. That Balaam's ass died after revealing the miracle of its speech prevented the worship of this animal for its extraordinary powers and spared its master the disgrace of people pointing to it and saying: "This is she that worsted Balaam" (Ginzburg 1972, p. 467). The ass—not Balaam's, but another's projection onto this animal—was to live on in another context in "The Rabbi Who Was Turned into a Werewolf."

The Werewolf/Rabbi's Shadow Transformed into the Hero's Companion

Meanwhile, when the hero returned to town with his companion, the werewolf/rabbi, the king as well as the entire community were terrified. Although he asked the hero to get rid of the vicious animal, his future son-in-law refused. Unafraid of the monarch's anger, he spoke out courageously and reasonably and, like Job, was adamant: "Your majesty, don't be afraid! He won't harm anyone if nobody bothers him. I'll put my head on the block for that." Although leery at first of the hero's stand, the monarch's faith in his young advisor's wisdom and integrity proved to be the right course. As promised, the hero was awarded the monarch's daughter as his bride. And the werewolf/rabbi, whose affection for the hero was demonstrated in many ways, was presented with fine food and drink.

When the king died, the hero, with the werewolf/rabbi always at his side, ruled with justice. Never did the young king forget that he owed to the animal not only the joy experienced in his marriage but his own life and also his kingdom. When happiness prevails, however, the wise person knows that flux is just around the corner.

One day, as the snow lay heavily on the ground, the hero and the werewolf/rabbi were indulging in a sport they both enjoyed: the hunt. The animal, running ahead of his friend and wagging his tail with glee, suddenly stopped and began grubbing in the snow with his paw. No sooner had the king arrived at the spot than he noticed some words written in the snow. Incredulous, he said: "There's something wondrous here—a wolf that can write! Perhaps he's really a human being under a curse! Such things have happened in the past!" Had the werewolf suddenly transcended his animal wrappings and become some "wondrous" entity?

Because the king could not decipher the script, he invited many scholars to his kingdom. Only one of them, however, recognized it as Hebrew and was able to read it:

> Dear king, remember our friendship and do not forget the good I did you when you came to my den in the woods. I could have torn you to shreds for I overpowered you three times. You certainly deserved it. But nevertheless, I spared your life. In the end, you became king. Know then that I have a wife in that town . . . and she put a spell on me. If I don't get the wishing-ring back very soon, I'll have to remain a wolf for the rest of my days. But if I can get back the wishing-ring, I can become a human being again like everyone else. Therefore I beg of you, recall my loyalty to you. Ride to that town, take the ring from my wife and bring it back to me for the sake of our friendship. Otherwise, I will kill you.

A sign in the form of a ring appeared at the bottom of the message.

Abashed by this turn of events, and despite the threat made upon his life, the king was faithful to his animal friend and set out to fulfill this latest task. The spark of self-knowledge, or the opening of his eyes, during his forest confrontation had served him well. Compassion, in addition to a sense of justice, would not only help him become a better king but would allow him to act in consort with his personality. No longer would he have to fight or repress his shadow, as he had when acting in accordance only with his arrogance-driven ego. Called into play at this juncture were the highest values and supreme consciousness—the attributes most desirable in a monarch.

The wise and mature hero now intended to help the one who had been instrumental in helping him experience fulfillment. Disguised as a merchant, the king set out with three servants for the town mentioned in the message in the snow. There he told the people of his intent to buy old-fashioned jewelry. After being informed of the whereabouts of a wealthy woman, he went to her home. In the group of precious objects she showed him, he happened to see a string of rings and recognized the magic one amid them. After buying two of them, just as the lady happened to look aside he stole the magic ring.

The monarch returned home, much to the delight of the were-wolf/rabbi, who not only wagged his tail but "flatteringly" kissed and caressed his Majesty. So touched was the king by the animal's show of affection that he withdrew the ring from his bag and placed it on the werewolf/rabbi's paw. No sooner did this happen than "a naked man" stood before the ruler, much to the shock and terror of the lords of the realm. To protect his friend from ridicule and embarrassment, the monarch immediately threw "an expensive cape over him to cover his nakedness." Moments later, the rabbi asked the king to grant him one more favor: to allow him to return home. Although the king was sad at the prospect of parting with his friend and invited him to spend the rest of his life with him, eating at his table, he understood the rabbi's desire to be with his people. They parted in friendship, mutually grateful for the kindness each had bestowed upon the other.

The Anima as Donkey

As the rabbi began his journey back to Uz, he gathered fifty students along the way. Prior to his arrival in town, however, he once again used the power of the ring: "I wish to God that my wife, damn her soul, would turn into a donkey. Let her stand in the stable and eat from the trough with other beasts."

Had the rabbi learned anything from his years of suffering and submission? Or could his regressive ways be compared to Balaam's subversive verbalizations at the conclusion of the biblical tale?

When the anima remains unconscious, as in the rabbi's case, and lives as a projection, the person involved relates to his partner in kind—as the carrier of the projection. Because no discernment has been shed on the problem of the rabbi's anima, he is bound to this "outer" autonomous power. Although his wife had won the first round of their struggle by transforming her husband into a werewolf, their extreme incompatibility had not ceased. The rabbi, however, was to win the second and final round in our tale. His faulty ruling consciousness had not, unfortunately, redirected his anger, thereby yielding to a more endearing anima image, which could have brought husband and wife together.

That the rabbi's anima figure, manifested at this time in the archetypal image of the ass, did not remain in the forest as he had but was relegated to the stable next to his house, is a sad commentary on his feelings toward his wife—perhaps toward women in general. In her residence in the stable, the rabbi would be able to make use of her positive attributes, that is, put her to work building a synagogue for the community. It was her job to haul bricks daily. So much exercise not only increased her appetite and made her fat, but, in keeping with the rabbi's anima projection, she comported herself as follows: "in front of people, she had no sense of modesty, she coupled openly like all animals." Perhaps annoyed because the donkey possessed the capacity to enjoy herself, the rabbi increased her workload. When she was tired, "he kicked her in the ribs and said: 'You wicked shrew! What ordeals you inflicted on me—the devil take you!' " Once the synagogue was completed, the rabbi gave a feast and told his entire story. Despite the fact that his wife's kith and kin pleaded with him to forgive her, he refused because he "wouldn't trust her." After the demise of the rabbi and the donkey, his wealth passed on to his children. As for the ring, it vanished as mysteriously as it had appeared.

What is the significance of the donkey that the rabbi should have wished his anima/wife to be transformed into one? A complex of opposites, depending upon the culture this animal represents ignorance, obscurity, sexuality, satanic powers, humility, wisdom, peace, patience, courage, and other attributes. This same animal, present at Christ's birth, was Jesus' mount when he returned to Jerusalem and was ridden by the most sinister Hindu divinities, such as Nairrita and Kalarati, as well as the Taoist Immortals. The ass has likewise been associated with the Beast of the Apocalypse. In medieval times, the donkey played an important role during the Feast of Fools, symbolizing a provisional reversal of values essential to the restoration of the egalitarian notions believed in by the early Christians. In Apuleius's *Metamorphoses* (or *The Golden Ass*), the hero, Lucius, is transformed into a donkey during the painful initiatory journey that takes him from a life of sensual delight into one of felicity and resurrection: his mystical contemplation and service to Isis. Most importantly, the ass was attributed by astrologers to Saturn, its qualities being compulsiveness, despair, suffering, imprisonment, and dehumanization (von Franz 1970, IV:5). The rabbi, aware that he can neither rid himself of his wife nor resume married life with this virago type, has her transformed into an ass, an image befitting the needs of his unconscious anima. As an ass, his wife will not only not pose any problems for him, but will also work in his favor by fulfilling his philanthropic needs.

And how does Balaam fare after his donkey has spoken? Impressed by the miracle of the speaking donkey, as well as by Balaam's ability as augurer, Balak takes him "to the high places . . . that he might see the utmost part of the people" (Numbers 22:41). As Balaam's gaze wanders over the camps of Israel, he tells Balak to build "seven altars" in honor of God (23:1). In ancient times, heights were considered conducive not only to prophecy but to astrological observation. Since Balaam is described as "one whose eyes are opened" (24:4,16) as well as by the epithet, "one whose sight is unblemished" (24:3,15), his words take on great meaning.[1] Just as the rabbi had a synagogue built to honor his God, harnessing his donkey/wife or anima to perform the task, so Balaam has "seven altars" constructed for the same reason. Rather than curse the Hebrews, he blesses the kingdom of Israel.

In like manner, the rabbi pursues his altruistic ways as teacher and as dispenser of food and money to the poor. Nevertheless, when it comes to making peace with his wife and revealing a compassionate and loving soul by returning her to her original shape, he remains unforgiving and, therefore, still tied to and victimized by that anima figure he fears to liberate. The same may be said of Balaam. Unlike Moses, who blessed his people in low tones, Balaam reaches out to the Hebrews in a loud prophetic voice, enabling other nations to hear his words praising their achievements. By arousing the envy of these nations, he also increases their determination to make war on the Hebrews. The blessings Balaam has bestowed upon the Hebrews are in reality curses, as he had originally intended them to be at the outset of his story.

The extreme ambiguity of both the Balaam myth and the rabbi werewolf story suggests humanity's continuous attempt to understand the mystery of existence so as to be able to alleviate or at least cope with difficult empirical situations. The magical bond existing between the two antagonists—the rabbi and his wife—took on reality in the form of autonomous powers (shadow, anima, animus) composed of unconscious psychological contents over which neither husband nor wife exercised any kind of rational control. If one or both had developed some kind of insight into the needs of the other, they might have been released from the stranglehold their shadow, anima, and animus exercised on their life experience (Harding 1975, p. 39).

When it finally spoke, Balaam's ass, considered the stupidest of animals, confounded Balaam, the wisest of the wise. In the rabbi's case, the donkey, associated with drivenness as well as suffering, compensated for his continuously destructive anima image. Ironically, it was the only way the rabbi, who was not in harmony with his instinctual world, could work with his wife. Unlike Balaam's ass, she would never answer her husband back, since she was deprived of speech; nor would she step aside in order to save his life. Although fundamental incompatibility lies at the root of "The Rabbi Who Was Turned into a Werewolf," the subtle and complex network of symbols used in the tale are appropriate in bringing forth a *modus vivendi*: as donkey, the wife feeds the husband's power drive and enhances his prestige while also working for the benefit of the community.

Note

1. Indeed, so significant were the words of an augur that ancient peoples, such as the Hebrews, Babylonians, Assyrians, and Romans, all consulted one prior to preparing for battle.

Bibliography

Edinger, E. 1978. *Melville's Moby Dick*. New York: New Directions.

Gaster, M., ed. and trans. 1961. *Ma'aseb Book*. Philadelphia: The Jewish Publication Society of America.

Gaster, T. H. 1969. *Myth, Legend and Custom in the Old Testament*. Vol. I. New York: Harper and Row.

Ginzberg, L. 1956. *Legends of the Bible*. Philadelphia: The Jewish Publication Society of America.

Harding, E. 1975. *The Way of All Women*. New York: Harper and Row Books.

Jung, C. G. 1970. The psychology of the unconscious. In *CW*, vol. 7. Translated by R. F. C. Hull. New York: Pantheon.

——— . 1959. The phenomenology of the spirit in fairy tales. In *CW*, vol. 9. Translated by R. F. C. Hull. New York: Pantheon Books.

——— . 1966. The psychology of the transference. In *CW*, vol. 16. Translated by R. F. C. Hull. New York: Pantheon Books.

Neumann, E. 1954. *The Origins and History of Consciousness*. New York: Pantheon.

——— . 1963. *The Great Mother*. New York: Pantheon, 1963.

Summers, M. 1973. *Geography of Witchcraft*. Secaucus, N.J.: The Citadel Press.

von Franz, M.-L. 1970. *Apuleius' Golden Ass*. New York: Spring Publications.

——— . 1988. *Projection and Re-Collection in Jungian Psychology*. Translated by William Kennedy. London: Open Court.

The Golem

A Recipe for Survival

The golem legend, a product of the Hebrew mystical experience, offers a psychological recipe for survival. To survive emotionally during periods of persecution, such as that experienced by Jews in sixteenth-century Prague, required the development of a religious view that would heal the scars left by harrowing oppression and instill hope in those who had lost it.

Before exploring the psychological meaning of the golem legend, a definition of mysticism in general, and Hebrew mysticism in particular, must be offered. Mysticism has been defined as the belief that one can intuitively know God or religious truth immediately and directly via an inward perception of the mind rather than through the usual route of understanding or sense perception. Mysticism has been linked with the Greek *mystes*, the initiated, thus with the Greek mysteries that were revealed to them. Thomas Aquinas considered mysticism as "the knowledge of God through experience." For Gershom Scholem, an outstanding scholar on the subject, the religious process involved in mysticism is the outgrowth of a personal experience during which the believer or the practitioner feels, tastes, and is aware of God. In the thirty-fourth psalm, we read: "Oh taste and see that the Lord is good" (verse 8). Mysticism, then, is a *unio mystica*: a union with Divinity. Some Hebrew mystics speak of the ascent of the soul to the Celestial Throne during the religious experience, the return to primordial unity, the annihilation or disappearance of the world of multiplicity. Mysticism exists in almost all religions; the particular forms of the experience, however, vary somewhat (Scholem 1961, pp. 3ff).

Although several varieties of mysticism are practiced in Judaism, they all share the notion of an "inner" or "higher" reality; the need to transcend the world of particulars or the world of contingencies: where everything exists in a state of flux; everything changes, diversifies, and multiplies. Hebrew mysticism, as evidenced by the prophets, psalmists, and religious practitioners, attempts to *know God* on a cognitive as well as on a feeling level. Of psychological significance was the restriction of mystical studies to small groups and to those already conversant with the Bible, the Talmud (the Jewish civil and religious law), and other solid religious tracts. Moreover, the Hebrew sages felt that only after the age of thirty-five should mystical tracts be studied. By that time, it was believed, wisdom would have made its way into the student's psyche; his feet would be solidly planted on this earth, and he would not be caught up in that "outer" world where his spiritual inclinations might lead him. In psychological terms, his ego would be safeguarded from the overwhelming upsurges of the collective unconscious.

Because mysticism was cultivated in small circles, its "secret" rites or rituals were guarded with fervor, passed on from "mouth to ear." Later generations called this "mystical stream" of Judaic gnosis *Kabbalah*—that is, "received" tradition.

The Hebrew word *golem* means "a shapeless mass" or "formless matter." In medieval times, this formless or shapeless mass came to mean a type of robot, or automaton, a kind of mechanical monster magically created. Although we are primarily concerned in this chapter with the golem of Rabbi Judah Loew of Prague, who lived from 1531 to 1609, he was not the first to create such an automaton.

Albertus Magnus, the thirteenth-century Dominican monk—a devout theologian, alchemist, and philosopher, and teacher of St. Thomas Aquinas—was also said to have been the inventor of an automaton. As such, he, too, attempted to understand the mysteries of life and matter. Whereas Albertus Magnus was trying to carry out God's will by perfecting himself and man, he was also, on an unconscious level—through alchemy—attempting to duplicate Divinity's act. He ardently sought to reach perfection—the *summmum bonum*—to become, in a metaphysical sense, the creator of the new man, spiritually oriented and pure. The biographer of Albertus Magnus, Joachim Sighart, postulated that Albertus Magnus had constructed one or several small mechanical figures that were able to make certain sounds, pronounce certain words, and move a few paces. The desire to create an automaton reveals a need to go beyond what is considered humankind's limited capacities: to be endowed with that Promethean drive that encourages a person to expand his or her knowledge, thereby leading to the discovery of the mysteries of the universe.

Roger Bacon (1214–1294), who was an English rival of Albertus Magnus, sought to learn extensively in order to better humankind's lot on earth and, by extension, his own reputation. He invented a "brazen head," he said, which is described in Robert Greene's play, *The Honorable History of Friar Bacon and Friar Bungay* (1558?–1592). In the drama, Bacon, the great mathematician and natural scientist, is pictured holding a magic wand and a glass. The brazen head says: "Time is, Time was, Time is past." Then, while Bacon steps out of the room for a minute, lightning flashes and a hand holding a hammer shatters the head. When Bacon returns and sees the destruction, he is disheartened: "My brazen Head is spoiled, / My glorie gone, my seven years study lost!" (Sandys 1914, p. 360).

Paracelsus (1453?–1541)—doctor, alchemist, philosopher, and for some, charlatan—not only created a *homunculus* but left us with the directions for bringing forth this robotlike entity. It was Paracelsus who said: "We are born to be awake, not to be asleep!" and "Therefore, man, learn and learn, question and question, do not be ashamed of it; for only thus can you earn a name that will resound in all countries and never be forgotten" (Jacobi 1973, p. 105).

We recall that in Goethe's *Faust* (act II, scene ii), Faust's aide, seated in his laboratory in front of an oven with its crucibles, says:

A glint, a living ember's glow.
Ay, as a burning jewel, the spark . . .
A light emerges, white and still:
This time an answer I implore.

Enraptured by the bubbling vials and chemicals before him, the aide speaks even more heatedly:

Now chimes the glass, a note of sweetest strength,
It clouds, it clears, my utmost hope it proves,
For there my longing eyes behold at length
A dapper form, that lives and breathes and moves.
My mannikin! What can the world ask more?

The mystery is brought to light of day.
Now comes the whisper we are waiting for:
He forms his speech, has clear-cut words to say.

The homunculus begins speaking from the vial.

Rabbi Judah Loew's golem, or automaton, differed from its predecessors. It did not come into being as a result of scientific research, nor was it a paradigm of humankind's vanity, that is, an attempt to compete with God's life-giving power. The golem that Rabbi Loew created emerged into the phenomenological world when the holy man was in a state of ecstatic mysticism—a soul in the process of ascending to Divinity. The golem answered a specific need for the Jews living in the Prague ghetto: survival!

Because of the extensive persecution of Jews during the Renaissance in most of Eastern Europe and in Germany (the projection of what Jung called "the shadow" onto a minority), a messianic figure was urgently needed to give the oppressed Jews the strength necessary to remain alive.

At the time, the Jews of Prague lived in a ghetto, that is, a section of the town enclosed by a separate wall and designated by law as the exclusive living quarter of the Jews. (The term is derived from the name of the Jewish quarter established in Venice in 1516, *geto nuovo*.) The gates to the ghetto were locked in the evening and kept locked all night. Suffering was great within the ghetto: there was poverty, there was degradation, there was persecution. Life, however, continued despite the hardships.

The creation of a golem fulfilled a need: its task would be to discover the plans for the extermination of the Jews of Prague and inform the community of the facts. Once the secret machinations afoot were brought to light, members of the Jewish community could then take action to prevent the further murder of their people.

The Origin and Background of the Golem Legend

An analogy may be made between the unformed mass of earth or clay from which the golem was fashioned and the earth (or ground; in Hebrew, *adamah*) from which Adam was created. In Genesis, we read: "And the Lord God formed man of the dust of the ground, and breathed into his nostrils the breath of life; and man became a living soul" (2:7). Had God not given his breath (*pneuma* in Greek; *ruach* in Hebrew) to Adam, he would have remained simply a piece of earth in human form, a mass of clay without a soul.

From earliest times humanity has attempted to imitate God's creative powers through occult or magical means. Stories of rabbis creating golems are recorded in the Talmud. Such feats were considered miracles that could be accomplished when the creators were devoid of sin. Never, however, in any of these legends is humankind's creative power equated with God's; rather, human inferiority is proven by the fact that something (usually speech) is always missing in the golems.

The mystical ritual that produces the golem is complex and is not based on any logical approach to Divinity. Like the creative process in general (literary, scientific, or artistic), it is based on intuition. During the golem-making process, the kabbalist (one dealing with mystical doctrines and rituals) sought union with God and attempted to experience His hidden mysteries. But no one dared attempt such a goal directly because the initiator would have been overwhelmed by God's power. In Jungian terms, he would have been overwhelmed by the flow of the collective unconscious, which would have blotted out, for the time being or perhaps forever, ego-consciousness. The kabbalist sought union with Divinity by means of certain rituals, or *containing devices*—by drawing on the energetic power emanating from words, numbers, letters, metaphors, and symbols.

The *Sefer Yetsirah* (*The Book of Creation or Formation*, first century C.E.) is one of those containing devices. It not only describes cosmic creation and ways for humans to share in it, but it also contains the golem-making formula. It is the earliest extant kabbalistic writing referred to in the Talmud and is believed to predate the second century C.E.—a time when Egyptian, Babylonian, and Greek mysteries were flourishing (Scholem 1961, pp. 75–6).

Because of the importance of the *Sefer Yetsirah* in our golem legend, certain aspects of it will be explained. That it is divided into six chapters refers to the belief that the universe is "sealed on all six sides with the six permutations of the name YHWH" (Jehovah); that there are "thirty secret paths of wisdom," which include the ten "elementary" or "primordial" numbers (referring to the *Sefiroth*, defined as God's Ten Emanations, or the ten expresssions of His "unfolding" into matter) and the twenty-two consonants of the Hebrew alphabet (Scholem 1961, pp. 76ff).

If we take into consideration what Jung wrote about numbers in *Psychology and Religion*, *Alchemical Studies*, and *The Structure and Dynamics of the Psyche*—and what Marie-Louise von Franz stated concerning them in *Number and Time*—we may look upon numbers, particularly when identified with mysticism, as being archetypal. Numbers, then, can be said to arouse energy, rhythms, and patterns and foment a dynamic process. They are "idea forces," that is, the concretization or development of virtualities or possibilities in space; they are also experiences or shapes that lie latent in the unconscious until consciousness experiences them in the form of "images, thoughts, and typical emotional modes of behavior" (Jung 1979, par. 870, and von Franz 1974, pp. 37–39).

In the conscious domain, numbers are *quantitative*; in the unconscious, they are both *quantitative* and *qualitative*, thereby arousing all kinds of sensations and feelings. As ordering devices used by humankind since the beginning of time, numbers are manifestations of a desire to conquer the world of contingency as well as the one that lies beyond it. In that numbers lend order to what might be considered chaotic, they give a sense of security to those in need of it and in this regard are considered by Jung as "archetypal foundations of the psyche." Understandably, an entire book in the Old Testament was called Numbers, for within its pages are enclosed generations of souls leading back to the beginning of time, thus giving historical continuity to the Jewish people. The tracing of Christ's lineage back to David is also an attempt on the part of a group to experience its ancestral soul in its original form.

The twenty-two consonants of the Hebrew alphabet, as disclosed in the *Sefer Yetsirah*, are believed to compose the structural elements of the universe and the foundation of the world. In the infinite combinations and phonetic divisions inherent in these numbers and "basic letters" exist the "roots of all things"—including Good and Evil. Since every letter and every number is thought to be charged with its own energy, each varies in power depending on its placement in the sentence or on the page, as well as on its meaning, sound, weight, and measurement. Analogies are made between each letter and the three realms of creation: the human sphere, the celestial domain, and "the rhythmic flow of time through the course of the year." The relationship between the function of Divinity and between letters and numbers is explicitly expressed in the second chapter of the *Sefer Yetsirah*:

He designed them, He formed them, He purified them, He weighted them, and He exchanged them, each one with all; He formed by means of them the whole creation and everything that should be created subsequently. (*Sefer Yetsirah*, p. 20)

Bloch's Version of the Golem Legend

Now that we have prepared the background material necessary to our golem legend, let us look more closely at Chayim Bloch's version of it (1920).[1] The narration is both terrifying and comforting: terrifying because it deals with man creating man, comforting in that it reveals the steps taken that helped a whole community survive persecution.

Bloch places his tale in the Jewish community of sixteenth-century Prague, a city described as "the home of sages, scholars, saints, and mystics; the scene of a thousand wonders, innumerable horrors." Every aspect of Bloch's tale radiates from one figure: the venerated and venerable Rabbi Judah Loew, referred to as the "Exalted One." The people's admiration of him was so great that they endowed him, unconsciously, with life-giving powers. Messianic figures, according to Jung, are usually characterized by miraculous deeds and traits. Judah Loew was no exception: even before his birth good omens were forthcoming.

As his father, Rabbi Bezalel of Worms, presiding over the Passover service at his home, began singing the litany, "It came to pass at midnight," his wife felt the first pains of childbirth. When several guests at the Passover feast ran for a midwife, they encountered a man in the dark, narrow street who was carrying a small bundle. Suspicion was aroused, and although he tried to escape, the night patrol caught him and took him to the magistrate. The man confessed that he had been paid by certain Christians, whose names he gave to the magistrate, to smuggle into Rabbi Bezalel's cellar the body of a Christian boy who had died the previous day. A search would then have been initiated, and the Jews would have been accused of murder for ritual purposes. (The thought behind such an accusation was that Jews needed the blood of a Christian to mix with their unleavened bread—matzoh—for Passover.) When the community realized that they had been spared another scourge of persecution, they gave thanks to God.

According to Bloch, Judah Loew had been endowed prior to his birth with a supernatural power of saving. His father stated:

"The child is our people's comforter. He has come into the world in order to free us from the terrible blood lie, the most ignominious calumny which we suffer." As the years passed, Judah Loew took on further qualities of a savior—so desperately needed by the Jews of Eastern Europe.

First educated at Worms, Judah Loew was then sent to Prague as was the custom, to continue his studies in one of the most ancient Jewish communities in Europe. After his marriage, this kind, compassionate, and humble man, this fine scholar and humanitarian, was asked to become the spiritual leader of the Prague community. He accepted, although he knew at the time that the priest Thaddeus, among other Catholic theologians, was still trying to incite the populace against the Jews through blood accusations. Aware of the existing dangers to his people, he asked to meet with the ecclesiastics of Prague to solve the problem.[2] He wrote to Johann Silvester, the cardinal of Prague, informing him of the accusations being leveled at the Jews—the injustice of which he knew to be opposed to Christian beliefs and therefore sinful. He also asked permission to "hold a disputation" with some of the priests, and the cardinal agreed. Rabbi Loew debated thirty times in thirty days, each time answering the questions put to him by ten priests. The disputations, Bloch informed his readers, are to be found in the archives of the Dominican Order in Prague.

First, Rabbi Loew explained the absurdity of the blood accusations, underlining the fact that "the use of blood is forbidden by the Holy Scriptures," whereupon he quoted from the Sanhedrin: "Whoever raises his hand against his neighbor even if he does not strike him is an evil-doer." Among many other arguments posited by the rabbi was the fact that the Jews, contrary to the belief of many Christians, were not guilty of Christ's crucifixion. "If," he stated, "Jesus died on the cross to save humanity, to do penance for its sins, He must, according to your doctrine, have suffered a tragic death with all of its bitterness and indignity in order to return as a sacrifice to his father. It had to be so, it was the unsearchable and indescribable decree of God." Had Jesus not sacrificed himself, "how could Christianity have originated, how could it continue to exist if its founder had not been a martyr?" Resorting to history, Rabbi Loew declared that punishment by crucifixion was not known in the Talmud but was introduced by the Romans. The rabbi then told an allegorical tale to further his belief in the innocence of the Jews: A king's only son had been accused of the crime of lèse-majesté.

A Recipe for Survival

Although the king was certain of his son's innocence, he did nothing to help him, nor did his son speak a word on his own behalf. Finally the son appealed to his father for help, but the king said nothing and he was condemned. Who was to blame for the unjust verdict: the judges or the king? The king, declared the rabbi, beyond the shadow of a doubt, because he could have saved his son with one word—just as, by implication, the "ruling" church officials could save the Jews of Prague by rejecting the distorted judgment of the populace.

The cardinal was impressed with Rabbi Loew's answer and said, "I hope from this time on peace and harmony will prevail between the adherents of both faiths." The three hundred priests who took part in the debate were also intent upon maintaining friendly relations with the Jewish community. Despite these hopeful signs, a group of anti-Semites remained, led by the priest Thaddeus. In 1580, with the help of others, he again charged the Jews of Prague with "ritual blood murder."

One night, Rabbi Loew had a dream which told him to make a golem in order to fight the accusations. The dream revealed how the chosen letters from the *Sefer Yetsirah* should be ordered and articulated. Rabbi Loew acted on his dream, but since, according to mystical law, a single individual is not empowered to create a golem, the rabbi sought the aid of two highly regarded men of his community. He said to them:

> I wish to make a Golem, and I bespeak of your cooperation because for this creative act the four elements Aysch, Mayim, Ruach, Aphar (fire, water, air, earth) are necessary. Thou Isaac, art the element of fire; thou Jakob, art the element of water; I, myself, am air; working together, we shall make out of the fourth element, earth, a Golem.

Not only did he inform them of the complex ritual and the purity of soul needed for the religious ceremony but also of the dangers involved. If by reason of incomplete inner sanctification "the Holy name" were profaned, he said, it would be a perilous desecration.

After midnight on the second day of the month, the rabbi and his friends fulfilled the prescribed prayers and purification rituals, then proceeded to the bank of the Moldau, where they fashioned the golem out of earth. Rabbi Loew then wrote the word *truth* (*emeth*) on its forehead, named it Joseph, and instructed it in its functions:

Know thou that we have formed thee from a clod of earth. It will be thy task to protect the Jews from persecution. Thou shalt be called Joseph and thou shalt lodge in the home of the Rabbi. Thou, Joseph, must obey my commands, when and whither I may send thee—in fire and water; or if I command you to jump from the housetop, or if I send thee to the bed of the sea!

After the newly created Joseph acquiesced by nodding its head, the rabbi took it home. He informed his household and community that Joseph was forbidden to fulfill any private or secular errand. This was an important injunction, for one day when the rabbi's wife asked the golem to fetch water, Joseph did such a bad job that the courtyard was flooded.

Most tasks were accomplished by the golem around the Passover season, thereby averting the accustomed accusations and round of persecutions. For difficult and dangerous missions, the rabbi provided the golem with an amulet to make it invisible if the need arose. Thus the golem could eavesdrop whenever suspicious characters lurked about the Jewish ghetto. Joseph often discovered infant corpses waiting to be placed in synagogues or in the cellars of Jews. (Sometimes graves were opened and children's bodies removed to areas that incriminated Jews.) The golem was ever present to rectify the cruelly unjust plots and to catch the culprits.

On one occasion, in 1584, while reciting prayers in his Altneu Synagogue, Rabbi Loew heard himself reading "and He *sours* the seasons" instead of "and He *changes* the seasons." The rabbi was frightened by this error, which he considered an evil omen. After meditation, he requested that the golem bring him an ordinary matzoh as well as one prepared for the Passover meal and then asked the golem to taste both. The ordinary matzoh was good, but the one made for Passover caused the golem acute pain. The rabbi immediately ordered the poisoned matzoh not to be eaten by the congregation of Prague. Thanks to the golem and the rabbi, the police chief apprehended the criminals, who had been paid by Thaddeus.

As the social and economic situation in Prague became less precarious, the need for the golem diminished. When one day Rabbi Loew forgot to outline the golem's daily task for him, the stored energy in the creature caused it to go wild, terrifying the community. "Panic soon reached the Altneu Synagogue where Rabbi Loew was praying," and he ran out to find the golem and told it to go

A Recipe for Survival

home to bed. He then returned to the synagogue and for the second time intoned the Sabbath Song (Psalm 92).

Rabbi Loew realized that the golem's constructive phase had passed. It "could have laid waste all of Prague" if he had not abated it in time. Hence he ordered the golem to sleep in the garret of the Altneu Synagogue, where at two o'clock in the morning Rabbi Loew and the two friends who had helped in the creation of the golem participated in its destruction. The ritual was executed in reverse, the golem Joseph's clothes were removed, and he was turned again into formless earth, which, according to custom, was covered with old prayer robes and remains of Hebrew books. The following day the rabbi announced that no one was ever again to go to the garret of the Altneu Synagogue. Bloch's tale ends on a note of nostalgia and hope: the memory of the golem remains, and it is believed that when there is desperate need, from this area a helping force does arise.

Psychological Implications of the Golem Legend

Rabbi Loew may be viewed as the archetype of the wise old man: a kind, fatherly, messianic figure whose presence is mysterious, whose powers are God-sent, and whose goal is to give courage. The golem may be seen as an archaic aspect of the "savior type." Both are instigators of psychic energy. The rabbi, as spirit, and the golem, as matter, form complementary figures and function harmoniously to greatly encourage the populace. They both inspire sufficient psychic energy in believers to enable them to survive through their own positive action, although frequent persecution besets them.

The golem's collective creation is significant in that its mission was to answer a collective need. On rare occasions, when ordered to perform a service for an individual, it did its task improperly. As the crisis gradually diminished (after Rudolf II signed the decree forbidding "blood-ritual accusations"), the necessity for the golem's existence also diminished. To allow its function to continue would have been dangerous for the community and for Rabbi Loew as well. Encouraging the community to rely upon others would have paved the way for psychological dependence and weakness.

Allowing the golem to live on indefinitely might also have placed Rabbi Loew in danger of hubris; a sense that he was capable of performing "miracles" and that his power could increase perpetually might overwhelm him. Such inflation could lead to "blindness'' from a psychological point of view—that is, a lack of spiritual vision that would endanger him and the community. When Rabbi Loew forgot to give the golem orders, he indicated that unconsciously he no longer needed the golem because the tension and fear caused by the crucial dangers had vanished—at least for the time being.

Rabbi Loew: A Positive Father Archetype

Rabbi Loew—like many doctors, priests, pastors, teachers, and magicians of legends, myths, and fairy tales—may be alluded to in Jungian terms as the positive father archetype. He filled an urgent inner need by compensating for the precarious life situation of the society that projected its cultural values upon him. Not only did he possess vital insights and determination but he was a planner of the future and discoverer of the difficulties and dangers that faced the community collectively. Although his intuitive faculties were keen, he could not cope with the situation alone because his resources were not strong enough. Deeply pained by the suffering he saw, he was able to summon an inner force, as Jung put it so well, and became ''a spiritual functioner.'' The result: unconscious elements within him were activated, and the ensuing emotional upheaval brought fresh ways of viewing situations. Because of his remarkable success, the community regarded him as a savior.

Every detail about Rabbi Judah Loew's life seems to emphasize his position as savior of his community. The name, Judah, itself, indicates courage, strength, kindness, and wisdom. In Genesis, we read of the lion of Judah:

> Judah is a lion's whelp: from the prey, my son, thou art gone up: he stooped down, he crouched as a lion, and as an old lion; who shall rouse him up? (49:9)

Like other outstanding father images throughout history, Rabbi Loew was associated with miraculous events. As already mentioned, his birth on Passover night (the night when Yahweh rescued his people from the Egyptians) inadvertently saved the Jews of Prague from persecution. That such a synchronistic event should have occurred on Passover night indicated the rabbi's symbolic association with Moses. Like his great predecessor, Rabbi Loew was to lead his people out of bondage, free them from the fear of annihilation, and teach them how to cope with their unfortunate situation. The ancient exodus from Egypt, a symbol of rebirth and renewal, was being relived by the Jews of Prague as an *imitatio Mosi*.

As an archetype of the wise old man and replica of Moses, Rabbi Loew stood for spirit descending into human consciousness. He symbolized the divine element functioning in humanity. When Loew's spirit became activated, it took on physical dimension as it focused on mystical letters and numbers of the *Sefer Yetsirah*. Because this document emphasized meditation, prayer, incantation, and bodily movements, it had become, to use Jung's words, an *exercitia spiritualia*, thus releasing inner energy. Once this energy becomes part of a person's conscious life, it may be channeled to confront outside factors.

The inner experience Rabbi Loew gained from practicing these religious techniques enabled him to apply his new knowledge to the dangerous situations around him. First, he listened to the voice of the transcendental force, or God (the Self), within him. When he attained this inner focus, the rabbi discovered the practical directives needed. Prayer (the contacting of Divinity) is a technique that permits expanded consciousness; when allied with incantation and bodily movements, it becomes a transformation ritual. As such, prayer transforms individual conflicts by releasing them to the collective sphere; it also diminishes the power of the rational function while enabling a concomitant encroachment of instinctual and collective forces. Jung suggested that the encroachment of such forces generates activity which enables the religious individual to experience a larger frame of reference because he is no longer limited to his everyday rational pattern of action. For Rabbi Loew, prayer was a dynamic agency, an autonomous factor leading directly to a heightening of consciousness that enabled him to transcend the mortal sphere and enter the fullness of an immortal realm.

Rabbi Loew never used prayer as an escape mechanism. On the contrary, it infused him with added energy distilled from his psyche, giving him the necessary power and vision to pursue his perilous course. Prayer organized his unconscious resources into conscious ones that could then be channeled into bold new lines of activity. Had Rabbi Loew's disquietude emerged without proper preparation, merely as an affect, it might have resulted in irrational acts or hysterical outbursts: he could have become a danger rather than a savior for his community.

The Golem: The Archetype of an Archaic Being

The golem is an archetypal image that emerges from the collective unconscious as an archaic being symbolizing instinctive telluric power. Because it had no soul, the creature had no will, no ego, no desires, no sexuality; it was a passive entity, a "clod of earth" whose function was to obey. The spark was lacking that makes human existence exciting and unique. In Chayim Bloch's words:

> There is no trace of good or bad instinct in the Golem, and all his actions are only like those of an automatic machine that fulfills the will of its creator. The Golem had to remain dumb because, as an incomplete creation, he was unworthy that the NESHAMAH, the light of God, dwell within him. He was inhabited only by NEFESH (sensory being and *Ruach*).

In that the golem was devoid of a soul, one might say that he had no life of his own. It is the function of the soul (anima/animus in Jungian terms), to arouse the individual to move into the mainstream of existence—into matter. Once he becomes part of the workaday world—the world of opposites—he cannot help but experience conflict. Then the individual's very struggle teaches him to differentiate between situations, feelings, and ideations; to evaluate circumstances and to function as an independent person in life.

When Rabbi Loew wrote "truth" on the golem's forehead (enabling it to function for the community), he was allowing a projection from his inner world to exist as a psychic reality. He then withdrew the projection at the end by erasing the word "truth" and reducing the golem to dust.

The twofold action indicates a recognition of the projection of "God" (or "truth") onto the golem object and a realization of the dangers involved if such an object persists beyond its time. The interdict from Abraham's time onward against making graven images had stifled Jewish psychic energy, or libido, in this respect. But when occasionally the need for a collective image did arise, it did so powerfully, as attested to by the concept of the golem. Nevertheless, after the need had passed, this interdict brought about the destruction of the golem, eliminating any tendency to worship it or its creator. As a crystallization of an archetype, the golem could have mesmerized the Jewish community. Thus the consciousness and aggressiveness needed to cope with life might have diminished.

The Traditional Ritual for Golem-Making Viewed as Psychic Therapy for Survival

The golem ritual is divided into six steps.[3]

1. The first step in the golem-making process as practiced by Rabbi Loew was generated by fear. His emotional response voiced the feelings of his people:

> I *fear* this Thaddeus [one of the persecutors of the Jews of Prague] for his soul is a *spark* of Goliath the Philistine giant. I hope, however, to subdue him, for my soul is a spark of the Jewish youth and later king, David. We must, nevertheless, all bend our entire spiritual energies to the end that we may not become his victim.

Fear, then, released an energetic reaction in the rabbi's psyche that altered his vision and transformed his activities and entire approach to life. The flow of energy was converted into an idea, then into physical acts.[4]

Rabbi Loew's fear was strong enough to transform latent energy into active force, indicating that his psyche was responding to inner tensions: the greater the anguish, the more powerful the energy and the greater the constellating power. Chayim Bloch cited David and Goliath as precedents: Rabbi Loew identified himself and his community with David, who, although small, won the victory over the giant Goliath. Rabbi Loew's battle in Prague had now taken on dimension; it had entered the collective sphere.

2. The second step involved Rabbi Loew's dream and dream-question. In the dream, he saw a fire raging across the street from the Altneu Synagogue. He directed his dream-question to heaven, asking for guidance and for specific instruction that would help him in his struggle against the overpowering forces of evil facing him and his community. Rabbi Loew's direct appeal to the Deity was in accordance with his religious nature. Psychologically, it indicated the tapping of an enormous transcendental power within him—the Self. Because this appeal took the form of a dream, one might say his energy was directed inward, forcing out contents from his collective unconscious (contents incompatible with the everyday world except in situations of great stress).

The archetypes that emerged from the rabbi's collective unconscious as images, if properly interpreted, could be helpful in dealing with the immediate empirical crisis situation. In general, as archetypes flow into consciousness they are accompanied by certain affects that cannot always be explicated along rational lines. Rabbi Loew experienced these affects in the form of impulses, intuitions, and perceptions formulated in what he understood to be God's dream-answer: "Make a golem of clay and you will destroy the entire Jew-baiting company." God not only told him to make a golem but revealed the necessary formula that enabled him to interpret the letters, words, and their numerical equivalents in the *Sefer Yetsirah*. As Rabbi Loew began his recitation, incantation, and meditation, the new emerging dynamism triggered feelings of sacrality and plenitude within him. The liberation of psychic energy he now experienced paved the way for a concomitant withdrawal of the ego (a function of the conscious mind—autonomous, to a great extent, during one's daily activities), and the new impetus constituted a progressive advance of the unconscious into the conscious sphere. The images emerging from Rabbi Loew's activated unconscious directed his perceptions toward associations with conscious realities, that is, those in the workaday world.

Psychologically, Rabbi Loew's dream and dream-question and answer elicited the positive participation of his unconscious. As mediating forces between the material and spiritual worlds, they helped him in solving his problems. Mystics term this process *an opening up to God*. Rabbi Loew had become the mouth through which the Almighty spoke. This kind of psychological experience seems to have inspired the historic prophets and messiahs. Their amorphous feelings or sensations were transformed into concrete images, their passive into active attitudes, their inert into kinetic energy. Thus it may be said that Rabbi Loew's psychic (or numinous) experience became a creative one.

Rabbi Loew had become a *nabi* ("mouth"), the harbinger of Divinity's message, as Aaron had been for Moses, chosen by the community to express the word of God and lead the people out of bondage.

It was Rabbi Loew's task to divine the truth hidden in the signs and the words formulated in the *Sefer Yetsirah*. In the process, he demonstrated the limitations of logic, adding to it a new, nonintellectual awareness of reality. *Thought*, the idea of an effective means to help his people, and *feeling*, his fear, coalesced in the dream vision. A concrete image of assistance entered reality for Rabbi Loew, and he would now "make a living body of clay."

After the dream-question had been answered, Rabbi Loew arranged these words in accordance with the formulas laid down in the *Sefer Yetsirah*, with the result that he was filled with the conviction that he would be able, with the help of the letters revealed to him from Heaven, to make a living body out of clay.

3. The third step was to call two other men to help the rabbi in the making of the golem. Kabbalists believed that at least two minds should participate in the study of sacred texts. These were considered to be necessary stabilizing forces for each other. If the ritual were enacted by one man, his unconscious might dominate and the mystic might lose himself in the undifferentiated sphere—in psychological terms, he might become insane. The two men Rabbi Loew requested to aid him were a Kohen and a Levite. The Kohens were priests, alleged descendants of Aaron, who performed ritual services in the movable tabernacle protecting the ark of the covenant during Israel's wanderings in the wilderness and later served in the stationary temple. The Levites accomplished the ancillary services of carrying ark and tabernacle throughout Israel's wanderings. Understandably Rabbi Loew chose these individuals, thus rooting his ritual in the structure of the dogma. From a psychological view, dogma is a protective device that holds within bounds the emergence of unconscious forces and thereby helps to channel their dispersion.

The number three, as applied to the participants in the golem-making process, is significant because, according to the *Zohar*, it defines three stages (*Kether, Bina, Chochma*) of the theogonic process (*Sefiroth*, or stages of divine emanation). Such numbers involved in God's emanations must be considered, psychologically, as archetypes or idea forces: each is endowed with a specific nature and tonality—with its own potentiality. All numbers emerge from *One*, the mystic state. The more differentiated they become, the more dominated they are by matter and the less powerful, energetically speaking, they become. Three is an active number representing the synthesis of two antagonistic forces; incomplete, it is in search of completion.[5]

4. The fourth step, symbolizing totality, introduced the earth element—the golem. The energy Rabbi Loew experienced in his *exercitia spiritualia*—always protected by and under the guidance

of dogma—could flow outward to be transformed into a concrete entity.

Three of the four elements (fire *aysch*, water *mayim*, air *ruach*, earth *aphar*) were represented by the participants: fire by Isaac, the Kohen; water by Jacob, the Levite; air by Rabbi Loew. To these three elements was added the fourth: earth, the golem. The names of the rabbi's co-creators confirm their functions.

Isaac (fire) was the only son of Abraham and Sarah and a sacrificial agent. As the fire principle in Rabbi Loew's ritual, he represented energy. The energy of the Jewish community in sixteenth-century Prague (manifested in their attitude) was not being used effectively. Neither strong nor well-directed, this energy had to be transformed to protect the Jews from persecution. Their way of life had to be changed or, symbolically, sacrificed. Transformation frequently brings what Kierkegaard calls "fear and trembling." The known, although horrendous, may be preferable to the terror aroused by what is beyond human comprehension.[6]

Jacob (water) in the Bible is known for dreaming of a ladder between himself and God. Water is frequently associated with the unconscious, a fluid potential realm—the *fons et origo* of existence. From Jacob's unconscious came feelings of belonging and unity with God, indicating strength, courage, and love.

Rabbi Judah Loew (air) represented spirit associated with divinity. As God breathed the breath of life into Adam, it was Rabbi Loew's function to give breath to his golem. Air is a higher form of matter, the symbol of invisible life and astral spheres.

Fire, water, and air acted together in the ritual—completing the incomplete and materializing a mighty agent to reverse an unjust power.

5. Penitence and purification, which made up the fifth stage, prepared the participants for "the exalted work of creating a being" out of clay. The disciplines activated the psychic energy needed for transforming matter from an inert to an active state, from the formless to the formed.

On Adar 2, an auspicious date,[7] the rabbis took their ritual baths, chanted the Hazoth, a "midnight lament for Jerusalem," and recited the psalm befitting the sacred occasion. Rabbi Loew drew out the *Sefer Yetsirah* and read the appropriate passage aloud. Then the three men walked to the Moldau River.

6. During the final step in the ritual, chanting by torchlight, the rabbis took clay from the riverbank and molded it into human form. Then Rabbi Loew asked the Kohen to circle the body counterclockwise seven times while reciting the prescribed words.

Seven is a number of particular significance. Its combination of three and four symbolizes a complete cycle, or order: the union of ternary and quaternary, the musical scale, the planetary spheres, the capital sins and virtues. Seven also represents the directions of space, the six sides of a cube (hexagram), or the six parts of heaven plus the seventh element—the center, which symbolizes Divinity. Seven is also considered a numerical reconciliation of the square and the circle.

That the Kohen walked from the right direction to the left is symbolic as well. The right side is usually equated with the rational or conscious sphere (and by extension with light, wisdom, sun, God), whereas the left side is equated with the irrational domain. The circular activity of walking around the body indicated that a new orientation was coming into being, a new frame of reference. (To walk around in a circle makes one dizzy, thus forcing upon an individual a readaptation to circumstances, an alteration of conscious attitudes.) As the Kohen rotated around the still-lifeless body of the golem, distinction disappeared in his mind; homogeneity of feeling came into being. The circle itself represents totality: the infinite, the Godhead, the Self. The Kohen was thus stepping into another dimension, another phase of existence—the suprarational or nonintellectual sphere.

As soon as the seven circles were completed, the clay body "became red, like fire."[8] Latent or inert energy was transformed into an active force. Fire indicates the presence of a supernatural power, and as such participates in the eternal mystery of death and rebirth.

The Levite's repetition of the Kohen's ritual caused a new development: "The fire-redness was extinguished and water flowed through the clay body; hair sprouted on its head and nails appeared on the fingers and toes."[9] Water functioned here as a cleansing and fecundating force causing growth.

Finally, it was Rabbi Loew's turn to circle the clay figure. He placed a piece of parchment in its mouth with the word *shem* inscribed on it, then bowed to the east, west, north, and south—the four cardinal points. Afterward the three men recited together:

And [He] breathed into his nostrils the breath of life; and man became a living soul. (Genesis 2:7)

The great moment had come: the golem opened its eyes and looked about in surprise. When Rabbi Loew told it to stand up, the creature obeyed. The three men then dressed it in the manner of an ordinary person, and the golem resembled other humans but was mute. At daybreak the four men went home. Before they left, Rabbi Loew told the golem that it was meant to protect the Jewish community.

The word *shem* (which gave life to the golem) not only stood for the name of God but also, psychologically, for the authenticity of a numinous experience. The truth of the vision (the unconscious fantasy image) had led to a creative act by the three men. Their joint projection had assumed life and functioned as a reality. The psyche, in this context, worked with matter and, when needed, transcended average perceptions. When the golem stood, inert mass became active mass, thus arising from dross to its higher form. The golem was made of earth, the feminine element. In conjunction with the masculine element (spirit), *tellus mater* had given life and in time would take it back again.

The golem was conceived as the outcome of an ecstatic spiritual expression. In time of great stress, people may—particularly if it is a question of survival—transfer or project their subjective torments onto some outer object. Once this occurs, the individual feels liberated from the turmoil of having to deal with his inner situation in secret; he is able to unburden his unconscious of incompatible contents. The identity between inner subject and outer object exists as long as this process helps to resolve the individual's plight.

During periods of dire crisis, such as occurred among the East European Jewry during the fifteenth and sixteenth centuries, the necessity to project inner stress onto some concrete image becomes essential. A messianic figure was therefore brought into existence. The idea of the golem came to Rabbi Loew after repeated arcane signs had been given him, as when he had a dream in which he saw a "fire" blazing across the street from the Altneu Synagogue. This sign and others the rabbi interpreted as God-sent warnings. Psychologists would say that the collective unconscious had revealed its awareness of dangers to the conscious mind of the Jewish community in the form of such dream images. These images were then reflected by the intuitive rabbi and acted upon overtly. His premonitions indicated that his unconscious had assimilated the elements of his external environment; after this, they coalesced as a single internal experience.

The question may be asked as to how the unconscious knows when and how to make its message known to the everyday mentality. Forgetfulness and lapses of speech indicate lost connections with the ego. Such disturbances suggest the intrusion of affects into the psychic process. As tensions in the unconscious mount, so does the energy inherent in the affected areas. The unconscious breaks through into conscious activity when it is most important for an individual to determine a new direction. Slips of the tongue and forgetfulness may reveal the individual's most profound secrets: they indicate a divergence between conscious and unconscious existence. *Lingua lapsa verum dicit* states the proverb. A speaker may make a startling slip of the tongue; this happened to Rabbi Loew when he misread a passage in the sacred text. Such a moment was "critical" psychologically because it indicated a high energy charge in his unconscious that set off a "spark" strong enough to disturb the smooth-running conscious intention. The uniqueness of the incident—correctly interpreted as significant—indicated to the rabbi that danger was afoot for his whole community. He was wise enough to act upon the insight gained from his premonition.

Rabbi Loew—a Promethean figure—and his creation of the golem are still potent forces in the minds of many. The possibility of resurrecting the golem in time of need remains a reality of the inner life of some groups of people even in the twentieth century. It is a human solution to an infinite mystery. As Bloch phrased it: *Mizad ze ruach chayim* ("For from this quarter the spirit of life flows").

Notes

1. Chayim Bloch was born in Delatyn, Galicia (1881). A member of a Hasidic group, he spent many years studying religious works, mostly mystical ones, and had become a rather successful businessman. When World War I broke out, he was already married and had several children. His physical state was so poor that he was not inducted into the Austrian army. When the Russians invaded, the Austrian government believed that the Jews would be shown no mercy and had them removed to Vienna. There, Bloch contributed to the newspaper *Wochenscrift*. He realized that little was known by the Austrians about Eastern European Jews—more specifically about the Hasidim—and decided to inform them of the Hasidic outlook. But by 1915, the Austrian government was in dire need of manpower and took Bloch into the army. He spent nine months in the trenches, became ill, and was finally discharged. Assigned duty at a camp for war prisoners in Hungary, Bloch met Jews from all parts of the world. He listened to their legends, enjoyed their humor, and noted much of what he heard on scrap paper. It was at this time that Bloch wrote "The Golem."

Bloch's version of the golem tale is a transcription of an earlier text compiled by Judah Rosenberg in 1909 that was based on ''an apocryphal manuscript in the library of Metz entitled: The Miraculous Deeds of Rabbi Loew with the Golem'' (Scholem 1973, p. 189).

2. Pope Innocent IV promulgated a protective bull (1253) with regard to the Jews, Rudolf I disavowed it, and Wenceslaus II (1300) reconfirmed it. The bull, listed on the books under the Hapsburgs, was adhered to by Ferdinand I (1527), but ''much arbitrary legislation was enacted because the Jews were considered enemies by the Christians. They were more heavily taxed than Christians; interference with their religious rituals was quite frequent; confiscation of goods and imprisonment were equally common'' (Baron 1965, p. 200).

An influx of Jews into Prague had occurred as a result of their massacre and expulsion from Moravia and Silesia (1453). Their contributions to the cultural and economic life of Prague were most impressive. In 1554, further expulsion of Jews diminished the Bohemian and Moravian communities. Despite the fact that many Jews succeeded in remaining by obtaining ''temporary extensions of their right of sojourn,'' the tension arising from their precarious position forced them to live in a state of constant anguish. In 1557, Ferdinand ordered another decree expelling Jews from his land. Extensions were granted under certain circumstances, but the situation was difficult. Blood accusations, charges of poisoning, forced conversions, high taxation, and interdicts as to the trades Jews could practice did not enhance their situation. Ferdinand's son, Maximilian, crowned King of Bohemia in 1562, decided upon a more moderate course. By 1563, he decreed that those Jews living in Bohemia could remain there and take up a trade. Rudolph II, Maximilian's son, was rather benevolent with regard to Jews (Baron 1969, pp. 157–162).

3. The golem-making ritual has many parallels with the alchemical process, which involved the manufacture of the philosopher's stone. Bloch tells his readers that during the reign of Kaiser Rudolf, alchemists and astronomers such as Tycho Brahe and Johannes Kepler were invited to his kingdom. It is known that alchemists had availed themselves of kabbalistic texts such as the *Sefer Yetsirah* and *Zohar* to help them in their experiments and calculations. They made free use of Hebrew letters, iconographies, and symbols, to which they attached their own arcane meanings (material, spiritual, sexual).

4. Such a notion may be explained as follows. The relationship between energy and mass is given in Einstein's equation: $E = mc^2$ (c is the speed of light).

5. Hebrews, Pythagoreans, Gnostics, kabbalists, and alchemists had their own traditions with regard to numerical symbolism; but in all of their beliefs, numbers represented a way of ordering chaos. Three symbolized the synthesis of two antagonistic forces.

6. For the alchemist, fire activated all other elements and paved the way for the transformatory process. Heraclitus considered fire an ''agent of transmutation'' and a symbol of regeneration. It represented the forces of light, radiance, and purification, spirit, and the sun. In Hebrew tradition, fire frequently alludes to the lamp (Exodus 27:20) that burned in the temple and symbolized God's presence among His people. Fire was the catalyst.

7. The day chosen for the golem-making ritual was Adar 2 (March). Its zodiacal sign is Pisces, and it is usually considered a festive month because the feast of Purim falls in it. The rabbinic dictum reads as follows: ''When Adar comes in, joy increases.'' Traditionally, Adar 7 is the anniversary of Moses' birth and death—or rejoicing and mourning.

8. Such alteration of energy seems also associated with the alchemist's *rubedo*: the fire needed to alter matter. The alchemist is always trying to reach a higher sphere: from putrefaction or mortification to the creation of the "seed of gold." The alchemical fire was no ordinary flame: rather, it was a "philosophical fire" that did not destroy the germinative power of the element but revivified it and resurrected it. Moreover, the alchemist's fire that burned in the *athanor* (oven) cooked the elements, enabling them to "digest" the substances and develop them, thus leading to their regeneration in other forms (Read 1937, p. 138).

9. Alchemically, the philosophical stone was being born: the *mystery* of matter embedded in the clay golem was entering its earthborn state.

Bibliography

Baron, S. 1965. *A Social and Religious History of the Jews*, vol. IX. New York: Columbia University Press.

———. 1969. *A Social and Religious History of the Jews*, vol. XIV. New York: Columbia University Press.

Bloch, C. 1972. *The Golem: Mystical Tales from the Ghetto of Prague*. New York: Rudolph Steiner Publications.

Capra, F. 1975. *The Tao of Physics*. Berkeley, Calif.: Shambhala.

Ginzberg, L. 1962. *Jewish Law and Lore*. New York: Meridian Books.

Jacobi, Y. 1973. *Paracelcus*. Princeton, N.J.: Princeton University Press.

Jung, C. G. 1959. *The Archetypes of the Collective Unconscious. CW*, vol. 9. New York: Pantheon Books.

———. 1960. *The Structure and Dynamics of the Psyche. CW*, vol. 8. Princeton, N.J.: Princeton University Press.

———. 1963. *Psychology and Religion. CW*, vol. 11. New York: Pantheon Books.

———. 1971. *Psychological Types. CW*, vol. 6. London: Pantheon Books.

Read, J. 1937. *Prelude to Chemistry*. New York: The Macmillan Company.

Sandys, J. E. 1914. Roger Bacon in English literature. In A. G. Little, ed. *Roger Bacon Essays*. Oxford: Clarendon Press.

Scholem, G. 1973. *On the Kabbalah and Its Symbolism*. New York: Shocken Books.

———. 1961. *Major Trends in Jewish Mysticism*. New York: Schocken Books.

Stenring, K., trans. 1970. *Sefer Yetsirah (The Book of Formation)* by Rabbi Akiba ben Joseph. New York: Ktav Publishing House.

Thieberger, F. 1955. *The Great Rabbi Loew of Prague*. London: The East and West Library.

von Franz, M.-L. 1974. *Number and Time*. Evanston, Ill.: Northwestern University Press.

Wayne, P., trans. 1979. *Goethe's Faust I and II*. Middlesex: Penguin Books.

The Dybbuk

An Alchemical Spagyric
Marriage

The Dybbuk (1916), written by Shloyme Ansky (Solomon Zainwill Rapaport, 1863–1920), is a religious mystery, a drama of possession and of eternal love. For the alchemist it is the paradigm of a "spagyric marriage": an inner psychic union that takes place beyond the physical realm, in a retort, as a projection. Psychologically, such a wedding acts as an escape from life into an atemporal world.

Alchemy is a science, a psychology, and a metaphysics. In C. G. Jung's words:

> The entire alchemical procedure . . . could just as well represent the individuation process of a single individual, though with the not unimportant difference that no single individual ever attains to the richness and scope of the alchemical symbolism. This has the advantage of having been built up through the centuries, whereas the individual in his short life has at his disposal only a limited amount of experience and limited powers of portrayal. (Jung 1963, par. 792)

Alchemy is also theater. As the twentieth-century theoretician of theater, Antonin Artaud, wrote:

> Theater is a mysterious identity of essence between the principle of theater and that of alchemy. Where alchemy, through its symbols, is the spiritual Double of an operation which functions only on the level of real matter, the theater must also be considered as the Double, not of this direct, everyday reality of which it is gradually being reduced to a mere inert replica . . . but of another

archetypal and dangerous reality, a reality of which the Principles, like dolphins, once they have shown their heads, hurry to dive back into the obscurity of the deep. (Artaud 1958, p. 48)

The alchemist transmutes his metals. The dramatist projects his yearnings and fantasies onto his play (his double) and, in so doing, alters their form and reality. In the psychological sphere, the unconscious delineates its contents in dreams, visions, hallucinations, and free associations, in the form of archetypal images and symbols of all types. In each of these domains, the realm of the unknown is encountered; it enters into being, acquires dimensionality, and becomes a dynamic force with which the creative individual must contend.

Alchemy offers many of its riches in the written records kept by ancient scientists: in iconographic representations, symbols, ciphers, and diagrams. Alchemists believed in the original unity of matter and in the possibility of its transformation and differentiation. What was of import to them was their ability to change impure leaden metal to a higher and more perfect Golden Essence. A parallel existed between their scientific activities and their metaphysical beliefs; as metals could be purified, so humankind could be elevated from dross to its spiritualized essence. Mystical notions concerning primordial unity, diversity in the manifest world, and the theory of correspondences and reincarnation were expressed in scientific terms—that is, in conjunction with chemicals and metals. First viewed as distinct substances, chemical combinations were observed to recombine under certain conditions and, interpreted from a mystical point of view, indicated a *coniunctio*, a union of opposites, an integration of antagonistic forces. Once opposing polarities were welded together, everything within the cosmos formed a cohesive whole, enabling a *renovatio*, a renewal, to take place.

The psychotherapist seeks to encounter the unconscious, to understand some of its contradictions and antagonisms as well as its creative élan. To transform what is negative into a positive and fruitful orientation or ruling principle of the personality is his or her goal. In so doing, the psychotherapist is elevating unregenerate matter (a leaden condition), or chaos, into a new golden sphere, or cosmos. If therapy is successful, the individual may work in harmony with himself and the world about him; he may remain independent despite functioning as a member of a collective society.

The dramatist also experiences a transmutation: from the unconscious (amorphous) idea that lies buried within his unconscious to the externalized incarnation that is his play; from the alchemical integration of disparate forces on the physical stage (actors, director, sets, lighting, sound effects, and more) to the realization of a new unity in the dramatic spectacle.

Before analyzing the dybbuk legend from an alchemical point of view, let us glance at the historical and religious situation of the Jews in Eastern Europe during the nineteenth century.

To survive emotionally the centuries of persecution the Jews endured, they had to develop a religious view that would heal the scars left by these harrowing conditions and instill hope in those who had lost it. Hasidism answered this need in many ghetto communities in Eastern Europe. Rather than focusing on earthly conditions, the Hasids emphasized a spiritual view, including belief in the transmigration of souls, joy in the service of God, and faith that a benevolent and blissful condition awaited the pure in heart and soul. The belief in transmigration of souls endowed individuals and entire communities with a sense of emotional and historical continuity, particularly when living conditions were as precarious as they were in the ghettos. The belief in the eternity of ancestral souls gave an archetypal foundation to the psyche. It was a protective device against the forces of oppression: to feel the presence of loved ones hovering about helped individuals overcome the very real terror of the pogrom eras.

The Hasidic sect reached out to embrace all those suffering, from the richest to the poorest, the healthiest to the sickest. It reflected the emergence of a new period: the age of the common man. As a mystically oriented creed, it accorded greater importance to the female principle than the strictly patriarchal Talmudic orientation.

The Dybbuk is based on a Hasidic tale. The word *dybbuk* means "an attachment." It represents the disembodied spirit of a dead person that has been unable to find rest. Punished for its sins (or those of the person or family it seeks out), this spirit longs for asylum in a living person and takes possession of that being. Stories of dybbukim date back to the Second Temple and to Talmudic periods, although the term itself never appears in the Old Testament; in the New Testament, it is referred to as an "unclean spirit." King Saul was possessed until the evil spirits were driven from him by David playing the harp (1 Samuel 16:14–23). The Essenes were well known for their miraculous cures of possessed persons. Christ exorcised demons (Matthew 8:16–31). Kabbalistic literature includes tales and "protocols" concerning the rituals to be followed in cases of exorcism. Today, the dybbuk would be likened to a case of schizophrenia, resulting perhaps from some unconscious psychic conflict dating back to a childhood trauma.

Although Eastern European Jewry suffered from the physical hardships and emotional problems resulting from nearly constant pogroms, the nineteenth-century Hasidic movement developed a rich spiritual and cultural way of life. The facts surrounding the life of its founder, Israel Ben Eliezer (1700–1760), known as the Baal Shem Tov ("The Master of the Holy Name") are shrouded in mystery. We know only that he was born in the western Ukraine, was orphaned at an early age, and spent many years in solitude and meditation near his hometown of Podolia. He studied the Talmud, the Torah, and the *Kabbalah*. After his marriage, the couple went to live in isolation in the Carpathian Mountains, where he continued his studies. He also immersed himself in nature, learning about the healing power of herbs and experiencing a veritable love for everything in God's world. Of prime import to him was the joy he knew when filled with the *Ruach Elohim* ("Spirit of God"), not the rigid theoretical laws set down by the Talmudists nor their casuistic discussions and abstract concepts. Every man could open himself up to spiritual elation, he believed, through meditation, prayer, and purity of heart. Rather than diminishing man's reasoning power, such moments of divine ecstasy would heighten them. Feelings of transcendence and of the unraveling of life's mysteries allowed the Baal Shem to see beyond the strict and immutable laws with which his contemporaries had structured their universe (Scholem 1961, p. 344).

The Baal Shem's teachings emphasized the heart rather than the head, the emotional rather than the cerebral. Furthermore, the *numinosum*, God's luminosity, could be experienced anywhere. Prayers need not necessarily be spoken to reach God's ear; they could simply be thought. Communion with the divine could be experienced through dance, song, and meditation, as well as the study of traditional Hebrew texts. What was essential was that the hierophant's heart be filled with love of God. Since God's immanence and omniscience encompass the All, nothing in the created world may be denigrated or considered completely evil. Although evil does exist in a variety of degrees, a person's function on earth is to redeem the wicked within the individual and the community at large (Epstein 1978, pp. 108–116).

Hasidism was a kind of revivalist movement which brought forth a new religious consciousness based on love, joy, and feelings of relatedness with God and with man. Rabbinical learning was not the main path to God; the *Kabbalah*, the esoteric and theosophical teachings of Judaism, were equally powerful. The most influential kabbalistic work was the *Zohar* ("The Book of Splendor"), comprised of mystical commentaries on parts of the Bible. These dated from the second century and were handed down in the form of discussions between Simeon bar Yohai and his followers in Palestine. Also included were the writings of the thirteenth-century Castilian scholar Moses de Leon and the sixteenth-century visionary, Isaac Luria of Safed. The *Sefer Yetsirah* ("Book of Creation"), ascribed to first-century mystics, and the *Sefer-Ha-Bahir* ("Book of Light"), one of the oldest hermetic documents revised and commented upon by Isaac the Blind in thirteenth-century France, were also important in the creation and formulation of Hasidism. The esoteric works deal for the most part with questions of cosmology, cosmogony, transmigration of souls, angelology, and demonology. Meditation exercises such as those implicit in the systems of *gematria* (giving numerical equivalents to words and letters in the alphabet) and *notarikon* and *temura* (interchanging letters and words according to certain rules) enabled initiates to understand the mysteries hidden within the lines: meaning preceding manifestation in the visual sphere.

Such religious devices stimulated new associations, fresh visions, and unheard-of spatial relationships in color, form, and sound, thereby expanding the way to Divinity. A new logic was discerned in kabbalistic teachings, no longer bound by linear time schemes or three-dimensional conceptualizations but experienced in a transcendental sphere. Various levels of consciousness were subsumed: lights could be heard, sounds seen, and the formless touched. The new values derived from these unlimited spheres served to transform worn concepts and give fresh interpretations to arid texts, new luster and dimensionality to the world at large. Disorientation frequently followed periods of expanded consciousness, but once the pleromatic sphere had become known to the mystic, an apprehension of God and his creation unknown to the intellect came into being.

The kabbalistic concepts of *gilgul* (transmigration of souls), *tikkun* (restoration of lights), *devekut* (mystical cleaving to God), and *kavvanah* (the intention), which were adapted and adopted by the Baal Shem, formed the core of his teachings (Scholem 1961, pp. 281–4). Gilgul may be understood as part of the kabbalist's cosmology and cosmogony. God's first creation, Adam Kadman (the primordial man), was an emanation composed of divine light. This essence was kept in vessels made of lower mixtures of light, which proved to be too weak to contain the force. The vessels shattered, causing these lower mixtures to scatter throughout the universe. God's next creation, the biblical Adam, whose soul held the souls of all mankind, fell into matter, alienating not only himself from God but also the whole of mankind thereafter. Once the earth became populated, it was incumbent upon each person to help restore the light to Divinity through the tikkun process. By means of this effort, individual souls would be redeemed. The tikkun may be initiated through devekut, a strictly personal view of life which implies "intimate communion with God." Devekut must be accompanied by kavvanah, an expression of the individual's sincerity (or "the soul of the deed") in the performance of altruistic acts that may lead to his union with the divine. If a soul is not redeemed after its first sojourn on earth, it may transmigrate three times thereafter, giving it further chances to fulfill God's commandment and its own salvation.

Gilgul, tikkun, devekut, and kavvanah pave the way for individual initiative, personal responsibility, sincerity, and faith in the divine. For the Hasid, God is within all beings and may be experienced by everyone, providing the effort is sufficiently powerful and the approach pure. To assure the Hasid of a balanced existence and some semblance of economic security, the Baal Shem taught that work in the existential sphere is of great importance. Families had to be supported, careers made, and futures determined. One could not spend one's entire life in a state of contemplation. The Baal Shem's emphasis on both the spiritual and physical aspects of life and on the accessibility of God through meditation, prayer, and acts, was indeed a comforting feeling for those whose lives had been terrorized.

It was at Vitebsk, Russia, his birthplace, that Ansky received a Hasidic education. Moved by the suffering and poverty of his people and humanity at large, he joined the Haskalah, a movement of enlightenment among Jews of Eastern Europe. Influenced by the political and economic doctrines of the Narodniki, a popular group, he decided to live among the Russian peasants. He worked at a variety of jobs until, in 1892, he was forced to flee Russia because of his political ideas. He went to Germany, Switzerland, and France, remaining in Paris for six years as secretary for Piotr Lavrov, a revolutionary philosopher. In 1905, he returned to Russia and joined the Social Revolutionary party, but spent his leisure time writing tales about the Hasid based on legends he heard around him. From 1911 to 1914, he traveled to numerous villages in Volhynia and Podolia, gathering material on the Jews as a people. It was in 1912 that he heard the tale about a young girl and her ghostly lover from an innkeeper. He noted it and later wrote his play. Ansky died on December 9, 1920, just a month before the successful opening of *The Dybbuk* in Vilna. His Yiddish works, which include plays, narratives, memoirs, and folk tales, were published posthumously (1920–25) (Kohansky 1969, pp. 32–34).

The Dybbuk

The events in *The Dybbuk* are so powerful, the feelings evinced so universal, and the characters so authentic, that the drama achieves mythical grandeur. The action takes place in a small Hasidic ghetto community or *shtetl*. It is here that one meets Channon, an ascetic student of the *Kabbalah*. He is poor and is in love with Leah, the only daughter of Sender, the wealthiest citizen in the shtetl. Channon tries through mystical rituals and theurgic practices to prevent Sender from finding a suitable match for Leah. Just as he becomes convinced of his power over destiny, Sender announces that he has found a husband, Manashe, for Leah. The shock is too great for the physically and emotionally frail Channon. He dies but returns as a dybbuk who captivates and haunts his beloved. The struggle waged by Channon's soul to possess Leah's soul is enacted on stage, as are the complex rituals involved in the exorcism procedures that lead to the play's deeply poignant conclusion.

As theater, *The Dybbuk* is unique. Contrasting spheres coexist on stage: life and death, the visible and invisible, the sensual and the spiritual, beauty and ugliness, ecstasy and misery.

Act 1: "White Fire on Black Fire"

At the beginning of act 1, the stage is dark. Low chanting infiltrates the atmosphere. An ancient Hasidic song, "Mipnei Mah," is intoned.

> Why, from the highest height,
> To the deepest depth below,
> Has the soul fallen?
> Within itself, the Fall
> Contains the Resurrection.

The lights brighten. The inside of an ancient synagogue comes into view. It is not only a house of worship but a meeting place as well. The walls of the synagogue are stained, "streaked as if with the tears of centuries." That it had originally been "built under the earth" in some remote era adds to its mystery. Miracles are associated with the synagogue: it was said that once the entire community had been destroyed by a fire and the synagogue alone was saved. When the roof caught fire, "innumerable doves came flocking down upon it and beat out the flames with their wings."

The table in the center of the *bima* (an elevated platform where the Torah is read) is covered with a dark cloth. On the side of the stage a wooden table is heaped high with books. Two candles are burning. A prayer cabinet near the Ark and an altar are visible. A half-dozen students are studying and chanting sections of the Talmud in low tones. At another table, the Batlonim, who spend their time praying, are in a state of near ecstasy. Channon, a young man seated directly under the Perpetual Light, is lost in meditation.

Moments elapse. The Batlonim begin talking about the wondrous tales and miraculous deeds of their rabbis. Mention is made of the "Original Serpent" Satan, "the enemy of God." The messenger, a stranger to the community, is lying on a bench near the stove. He sets the tone of the play when he says, "Only the heat of a too intense desire can cause the vessel to burst when the spark breaks into a flame." It is the messenger, like the ancient Greek chorus, who reveals unknown forces at work. He acquaints spectators with the reigning signs and symbols and also warns of imminent danger.

Fire is that force which caused the vessels enclosing Adam Kadman to shatter. Thus did the sparks of divine light scatter throughout the world of matter and fall into the "abyss" of life, starting in this way "the great cosmological drama" (Scholem 1961, p. 267). Since that time, everything in the manifest world has been imperfect, deficient, and unbalanced. Man's goal in life is to restore these sparks to Divinity, to repair the flaw through piety, virtue, and obedience to God's commandments. When light and flame become too intense to be controllable, as they were in Adam Kadman's case, they sear, destroy, and annihilate. As a sacred force implicit in Divinity, fire represents man's flaming desire or quest for spiritual and intellectual evolution, transforming itself into an instrument of regeneration and purification. For the alchemist, fire melts metals and creates new alloys: it makes the fixed fluid, boils the cold, and reddens the white. Its emotional equivalent indicates passionate need, volatility, activity, and intensity.

Channon, who has not budged until now, suddenly rises. He asks the Batlonim the whereabouts of those miracle workers whose wonders they have been relating. What are the spells they utter and the incantations they recite? The theurgic rites they practice? Where are these men who can resurrect the dead, cure the tormented, and bring joy to the disheartened? They live, Channon is told, in distant, inaccessible areas.

The audience now learns that Channon had once been a brilliant student. He was said to have a brain of steel and to have memorized five hundred pages of the Talmud. Moreover, strange things had happened to him. After receiving his degree from the yeshivah, he vanished. Some people said he had spent a year doing the "penance of the Golos," consisting of mortification of the flesh and wandering throughout the world as a beggar, helping others to gain redemption whenever and wherever he could. Upon his return to town, he had changed completely. Absorbed in meditative practices, he spent his time fasting, performing holy ablutions, and studying the *Kabbalah*.

Prayer, recitation, incantation, and swaying allow the mystic to experience various spheres of God's creation: different levels of his unconscious. It was believed that by concentrating on each word, the initiate opened up the way to inner light, which in turn illuminated more profound universal secrets, linking man even more strongly with the divine world. One of the main differences between Christian and Jewish meditative practices is the former's anthropomorphic visualizations. Concrete images of a suffering Christ, martyr, or saint appear during moments of divine ecstasy, whereas the kabbalist experiences his meditation in a world of abstractions—secret letters, words, and numbers. Their combinations and permutations are outer coverings for an inner awareness. It is the inwardness of the meditation that serves to attach man to God and enables him to open up to universal rhythms and become attuned to Him (Scholem 1973, p. 372).

Exhausted from his fasts and the intensity of his prayers, Channon walks toward the Ark, which houses the Torah. All "secrets and symbols" are hidden within these holy scrolls, he says. "All miracles—from the six days of creation, unto the end of all generations of men. Yet how hard it is to wrest one secret or one symbol from them—how hard!" Why does the number thirty-six invade his mind so constantly, he wonders. What is its essence? According to the mystical science of gematria, thirty-six stands for Leah; three times six stands for Channon. Tormented, he knows he must divine the secrets and symbols in these numbers and put them to good use.

The system of gematria is similar to meditation, incantation, and prayer in that it is a ritual designed to place the initiate in tune with universal forces and open him up to an influx of divine light. Numbers are archetypal forces. For psychologists and alchemists they are idea forces—that is, they are outer garments containing inner meanings. For Pythagoras they were a means to order chaos, render the infinite finite, and transform the amorphous into matter. The number thirty-six, a combination of three (the triangle, trinity, Hegelian synthesis) and six (a union of two triangles, as expressed in the alchemical theories of fire and water; the six days of Creation), indicates mysterious sets of correspondences at work in the universe. Why should Leah's and Channon's names be linked? Why should there be thirty-six Lamed Vovs, those men who, according to Hebrew mystics, lived painful existences hidden from the world, and who appear only in times of dire stress to reveal God's secrets to the multitudes? Perhaps Channon is a Lamed Vov?

The more Channon delves into the mystery of numbers, the more firelike his personality becomes. As archetypes, numbers are "structured contents of the collective unconscious" and therefore endowed with energy, dynamism, and the capacity to activate the minds and psyches of those who approach its mysteries (von Franz 1974, pp. 33, 53). When numbers detach themselves from the collective unconscious and enter into consciousness (in the manner of ideas or sensations), the image they form is imbued with a force that sheds its inner light during the course of its trajectory in the mind's eye. Like the alchemist's scintillae or his athanor, in which the coals purify the most ignoble metals and precipitate the most inert substances, so Channon's spiritual energy knows no bounds. For him the goal justifies the means. Passion continually pushes him to extract God's boundless mysteries from the universe for his own private use. Dangers await such attitudes, warns the *Kabbalah*. Catastrophes may follow. If spirit and mind grow too powerful for the body containing them, a split may ensue, as in the case of Adam Kadman. On a human level, disharmony and discord between soma and psyche may come to pass. The word *steel*, used to describe Channon's powerful brain, denotes, according to hermetic tradition, transcendent toughness of spirit. The hardness of steel, however, depends on the degree to which it is alloyed with other metals. Steel may also be malleable. So Channon, fired with desire, might either possess obdurate, stubborn, and insensible characteristics or simply display a fundamental weakness of character. All depends on the kavvanah, the purity of his spirit and the authenticity of his love for God.

Channon, whose spiritual and biological drives are manifest in the power of his fantasies, has become driven by his desire to dominate his destiny. He has, in effect, rejected the world of contingencies in which people are to a great extent victimized by forces beyond their control. He is no longer the pure, steely, shining student he once was. His soul has become contaminated, tarnished. The scintillae, once focused on Divinity, are now attracted elsewhere. Confusion has set in. Values have altered. Channon is unaware of the dangers awaiting the individual who misuses knowledge. The alchemist has always stressed the word *contamination*, indicating that the impurities within the metal lower its efficiency and may bring about the failure of the experiment. So Channon's flaw, reminiscent of Adam Kadman's, may lead to his diffusion into space.

A young scholar who has remained in the synagogue asks Channon why he has been delving into the *Kabbalah* when he knows its teachings have been forbidden. Only the initiated may study Kabbalah, and even for them it is not recommended. The Talmud gives structure and protection, containing the mind and allowing thoughts to proceed in an orderly manner, through discernment, logic, and reason. The Talmud is "cold and dry," Channon answers. It does not activate spirit nor does it fire energy. It stands for casuistic thinking, cerebral argumentation. Although the Talmud "is deep and glorious and vast . . . it chains you to the earth—it forbids you to attempt the heights."

A fire principle, Channon is incapable of proceeding temperately. He has always put himself through the most excruciating mental and physical exertions to experience religious ecstasy. Under the spell of God's presence, the rational world dissolves; emotions are allowed to invade his being. Psychologically, Channon's subliminal depths hold full sway. His weakened ego (that factor within the psyche that adapts to both outer and inner worlds) falters and then stumbles, rendering his already unbalanced existence even more precarious. Channon has become a spiritual cripple, unable to distinguish reality from fantasy; he is unable to adapt to a harmonious interplay between conscious and unconscious spheres. The *Kab-*

balah, Channon explains, "tears your soul away from earth and lifts you to the realms of the highest heights. Spreads all the heavens out before your eyes, and leads you directly to pardes [paradise], reaches out in the infinite, and raises a corner of the great curtain itself."

As Channon speaks of his ecstasy, he grows weak. Like the mystic who ascends to vertiginous heights, Channon becomes dizzy. *Sublimatio* dominates the scene. Vaporous and disembodied, his soul has become a distilled essence; the fire that generates and regenerates paves the way for communion with Divinity. When the intense spiritual quest serves only the individual, however, and not humanity at large, the flame lighting the way may blind or burn the initiate.

The scholar again warns Channon of the dangers that "ecstatic flights into the upper regions" may provoke. It is during such moments of rapture that souls are lost, burn themselves out, and then are hurled "into the deepest pit below." The slow and sure way of the Talmud "raises the soul toward the heights by slow degrees, but keeps guard over it like a faithful sentinel who neither sleeps nor dreams." It "clothes the soul with an armor of steel and keeps it ever on the straight path." As the alchemist protects his metals from contamination and corrosion in alembics and crucibles, so the ego, psychologically, must be restrained from powerful eruptions from the collective unconscious.

Unless properly initiated, students of the *Kabbalah* may be overwhelmed by its mysteries and blinded by the divine light streaming into the soul. Rather than purifying under these conditions, the Kabbalah may pervert; instead of instilling the hierophant with humility, it may fill his heart with hubris. Revelations that only belong to the most revered of prophets, such as Elijah, are never divulged to the ordinary being. Frequently, however, when inexperienced individuals arrogate unto themselves that which belongs to the immortal realm, they may be duped into believing that they possess powers over both material and spiritual worlds. The practitioner of theurgy, unlike the true student of *Kabbalah*, overreaches himself, wants too much, imagines too fervently, and divines too viscerally. If passion is allowed to burn uncontrolled, the wisdom gleaned from these sacred texts may be misapplied and destruction may ensue (Scholem 1971, p. 348).

Channon's kabbalistic studies raised him to a state of grandeur. Unable to understand the power of its mysteries, he felt so energized that he believed himself imbued with almost supernatural powers. Such feelings drew him away from the workaday world and divested him of any sense of obligation to or connection with his surroundings. As the ancient adage explains, "Whoever is full of himself has no room for God" (Scholem 1961, p. 132). Channon refuses to listen to the scholar. "I go my own way," he states. From time immemorial, holy men have waged fruitless battles against sin, Channon continues. No sooner do they cleanse one soul than others, more sinful, appear to plague the world. He seeks "to burn its sin away, as the goldsmith refines gold in the powerful flame; as the farmer winnows the grain from the chaff. So must sin be refined of its uncleanness, until only its holiness remains."

Channon identifies with the goldsmith, as had the alchemists of old. He sees himself as a flame burning and purifying the ignoble leaden condition until it reaches the sublime Golden State. Gold and light are synonyms for Channon. The Latin word (*aurum*) is the same as the Hebrew word (*aor*) meaning light. In his own mind, Channon has become a combination of solar light and divine intelligence and inhabits the fourth dimension. Gold, as the supreme spiritual value, is an elusive treasure and igneous force. Unlike the true alchemist, who knew that making gold required slow gestation, Channon rushes forward, unthinking, driven by the power of his inner energy. Pliny wrote that to gather gold, which is found in running streams and in grains in the earth, requires periods of sifting and purification (Stillman 1924, p. 56). The process of extracting the ore from the earth is arduous and long. So it is for the one seeking individuation and for the kabbalist as he wrests the mysteries from the pleromatic spheres. Only after years of study, meditation, and profound understanding can he even begin to approach his goal.

Channon tells the terrified scholar that sparks of holiness exist in sin. God created the entire cosmos. After the shattering of the vessels and the dispersion of Adam Kadman, the holy sparks were scattered throughout the universe. Just as these luminosities must be gathered and cleansed of the evil or matter with which they are encrusted, so must sinful thoughts be examined, understood, and thereby divested of their contamination; thus may evil be transformed into good. The scholar is thunderstruck. Satan created sin, he counters, not God. Channon answers by asking who created Satan. "God. Since he is the antithesis of God, he is an aspect of God, and therefore must contain also a germ of holiness."

Certain mystics believe that in order to rescue the divine sparks from the material world and return them to their source, a descent "through the gates of impurity" is required. Once such a task is completed, the "Kingdom of Evil" vanishes, since it no longer has a reason to exist (Scholem 1975, p. 306).

Evil exists only when good remains a dynamic factor. To descend into the domain of impurity, however, entails great danger. The initiate must identify with evil, thereby justifying his perversions. He may never be able to detach himself from this leaden condition. If he succeeds in returning to the Kingdom of God, he has earned redemption more so than those who have not sinned.

Redemption through sin is Channon's way. For him, it means a descent into the domain of evil followed by an elevation. In Ezekiel (33:11), evildoers are pardoned: "Say unto them, as I live, saith the Lord God, I have not pleasure in the death of the wicked; but that the wicked turn from his way and live; turn ye, turn ye from your evil ways." To prove his point, Channon says that the most powerful sin for woman is lust. Yet when this sin is cleansed in a "powerful flame," it achieves the greatest holiness of all in the Song of Songs. Channon begins chanting Solomon's love verses rapturously.

The Song of Songs occupies a very special place for kabbalists and alchemists. The former understood Solomon's verses allegorically, both as a mystical union between man's soul and God and between the community of Israel and the spirit of God. The text contained elements of God's sublimity and mystery, and those who felt it deeply could be transformed and renewed when chanting the poem or meditating on its mystical meaning.

The Christian philosopher Origen (185–254), who taught in Alexandria and Caesarea, wrote that in Jewish circles the study of the Song of Songs was forbidden to the young. No one knows the reason for the interdict, although many suggestions have been forwarded. Some feared the student might interpret Solomon's verses as erotic love poems between bride and bridegroom and therefore concentrate on base sexuality rather than directing their thoughts toward divine realms. Others, such as Maimonides, suggested that the anthropomorphism inherent in the *Shi'ur Komah* ("Dimensions of Stature"), a mystical work in which God's greatness was expressed by attributing to Him human dimensions and that was anathema to Hebrew tradition, might be interpolated in the Song of Songs. God is beyond human comprehension and may never be reduced to form. Still others, however, defended the *Shi'ur Komah*, which they compared in beauty and feeling to the Song of Songs. They were convinced that both books were allegorical interpretations of God and His "Glory," his *Shekinah* ("the body of the Divine presence" or, according to some, the female element in God). The Song of Songs was therefore considered to express God's longing for union with His Shekinah, referred to as the "beloved" (Song of Songs 5:11–16); in the *Shi'ur Komah*, God's "tunic" and "garment" refer to the "garment of light" which He donned when He created the world.

The alchemist views the Song of Songs in terms of its colors: red, white, black, purple, silver, and gold. Each hue represents an alchemical operation. The beloved is "black but comely" (1:5) and is compared to both a rose and a lily. The *nigredo* and *albedo* processes are embedded in her countenance and have metaphysical and psychological analogies. Comparable to a redeeming queen figure, the beloved possesses warmth and tenderness, understanding and love. She spreads joy and a passion for life. The shadow, her other side, however, which is associated with the dark, moist moon forces, ushers in warlike, chthonic qualities which spread madness among her followers. The beloved then becomes a poisoner when she emerges from darkness and extracts man's soul; she is an unredeemed force of nature that sets the alchemist on the wrong track. In the Song of Songs, she has both positive and negative aspects as sister, bride, mother, and spouse, and she may therefore bring him renewal, regenerating in this manner the alchemical process, or death. As the force of *renovatio*, she becomes the archetype of life itself (Scholem 1973, p. 49).

Unaware of the immensity of his undertaking, Channon interprets the riches hidden in the kabbalistic works in general and in the Song of Songs in particular on a personal, not a transcendental, level. Events in the outer world are viewed as a confirmation of his power over destiny. The fact that Sender is unable to find a suitable husband for Leah is positive proof, he believes, of his feelings. One day, he is certain, she will be his.

The congregation returns. Leah, a young and gentle girl, enters. She is accompanied by her grandmother. She walks over to the Holy Ark. Channon cannot take his eyes off her: "He alternately gazes at her thus and closes his eyes in ecstasy." Leah sees him and "lowers her eyes in embarrassment." Leah, the "beloved" for Channon, is an anima figure. She personifies the feminine principle in Channon, unconscious qualities embedded within his own soul which he transfers to her. It is she (through projection) who has altered his character and aroused powerful reactions. Channon has become so dominated by his soul-image Leah that he cannot adapt to real life. He lives inwardly. His libido is repressed. Every now and then, it explodes in the form of affects—as an ecstatic prayer or a power drive. She has no real relationship to Channon; she is not the product of a harmonious union between soma and psyche, or spirit and soul. Dissociated, Channon can find some semblance of solace from an abrasive world of reality only through the projection of this archaic identity with the soul object.

Leah looks at the "tear-stained walls" of the synagogue. Why are they "so sorrowful, and so wrapped in dreams . . . so silent and so sad. I wish . . . I don't know what I wish. . . . But my heart is filled with tenderness and pity." Leah wonders why Channon is so pale and sad. She looks at his "wonderful eyes." They are like diffused luminosities, flowing streams of light, nonmaterial scintillae emerging from some etheric realm. He is fire. She senses his power. Feelings of uneasiness invade her being. She kisses the Torah and is told not to kiss it too long because it is "written in black fire upon white fire."

The Torah is a living organism for the Jew. It preexisted creation in the form of "black fire on white fire." In this nonmaterial condition, it burned before God. The commentary on the *Book of Bahir*, written by Isaac the Blind, states:

> The form of the written Torah is that of the colors of white fire, and the form of the oral Torah has colored forms as of black fire. And all these engravings and the not yet unfolded Torah existed potentially, perceptible neither to a spiritual nor a sensory eye, until the will [of God] inspired the idea of activating them by means of primordial wisdom and hidden knowledge. (Scholem 1973, p. 49)

The written Torah could become manifest only through the power of the oral Torah, since "the white fire is the written Torah, in which the form of the letters is not yet explicit." The letters on the scrolls are merely limited material manifestations of the primordial, amorphous, and unlimited word of God. Its meaning, therefore, is no longer concealed in the white and black light but is structured and limited, its essence remaining inaccessible to man. For Leah to allow her kisses to remain too long on the Torah would be as dangerous to her well-being and equilibrium as is the study of esoteric literature to the uninitiated. She might intuit the "inwardness" of each letter; its spiritual message would therefore invade her being like lighting, energizing and stimulating her adolescent orientation.

After Leah's departure, Channon, as though intoning to himself, concentrates all of his energies on the pronunciation of certain words. He seems to be growing desperate. "I wish to attain possession of a clear and sparkling diamond and melt it down in tears and inhale it into my soul. I want to attain the rays of the third plane of beauty. I want . . . ." The "third plane of beauty" is to be found, according to mystics and alchemists, in Solomon's writings: the Song of Songs represents the sphere of Beauty, Ecclesiastes represents that of Judgment, and Proverbs represents that of Loving Kindness (Epstein 1978, p. 59). Only after he has experienced the three may the "diamond" appear for the mystic, the philosopher's stone come into being for the alchemist, and the individuation process pursue its course in the psychological domain.

That Channon seeks "to attain possession of a clear and sparkling diamond" indicates his longing to enter the domain of the absolute, to be bound to Leah. As an anima figure, she is, as far as he is concerned, the essence of pure divine light. In Sanskrit, the word *dyu* ("diamond") also means "luminous being," "light," and "brilliance" and is connected with the Greek word *adamas* ("unconquerable"). The mystic and alchemist both seek the diamond or the treasure hard to attain, that irradiant center from which moral, spiritual, and intellectual values emerge. To possess the diamond or to create it—or to realize it in one's own being—is an extremely difficult task. The diamond, like man's moral attributes, ranges from the most impure to the purest of states. A naturally crystallized diamond is one of the hardest substances known, but in its uncrystallized form it is opaque and frangible. To seek out the diamond requires excavation; arduous polishing is necessary to perfect it and bring out its hidden light and luster. So the alchemist must likewise indwell, discover the diamond existing within, force it out of its darkened recesses, and then perfect it through the various stages of the evolutionary process until it emerges shining in its sovereignty and incorruptibility.

Channon's renegade tendencies do not allow him sufficient time to divine the mysteries of matter or to understand the human experience. As a fire principle, he plunges into the pleromatic sphere, into his unconscious, and there escapes from the difficulties involved in dealing with reality. In so doing, he rids himself temporarily of his feelings of inadequacy. Although a fire principle, he is not a solar hero whose courage knows no bounds and whose heroism can move mountains. Channon works in darkness, in unconscious and instinctive areas. His ego is never perceptible; on the contrary, it is underfed, limp, and dwindles progressively in strength, eventually removing him completely from any sense of responsibility. His longing to reach out and possess his beloved Leah inspires him to forge ahead in his mystical quests. His connection with her, however, exists only in his mind. As his fantasy gains power over him, he withdraws still further from the workaday domain. Filled with poetic rapture, which he mistakenly interprets as an influx of divine energy, Channon believes that Leah's love for him has made him whole again: she has given him the warmth and tenderness he had never known in life. By submitting to such an obsession, however, Channon has severed relations with society. His life, therefore, cannot be renewed or nourished through positive contact with his instinctive depths, since these are now in full sway. Dangers encroach. Conscious values have been lost and his individuality drowned within the limitless sphere of the collective unconscious. Only alienation can ensue.

Channon grows desperate. Nothing seems to be working: not his fasts, his ablutions, nor his spells. Perhaps "the Secret of the Double Name" can come to his aid, he thinks. Mystics believe that initiates may divine the original texture of God's name, "by which heaven and earth were created," according to certain permutations and combinations of letters and formulas. But the pronunciation of the four sacred letters YHWH (the Tetragrammaton) is no longer known to man. Channon's inflated ego allows him to believe that meditation, concentration, and prayer will enable him to discover them. But as is stated in Job (28:13): "Man knoweth not the price thereof; neither is it found in the land of the living." No one may discover what preexisted the world; no one may understand "the secret life of God." As the thirteenth-century Spanish kabbalist Joseph Gikatila explained: "Know that the entire Torah is, as it were, an explication of, and commentary on, the Tetragrammaton YHWH" (Scholem 1973, p. 43). Woven into the very fabric of the Torah is the secret leading to the understanding of the oral and written Torah, "black fire on white fire." Only Moses understood its "hidden and invisible form in white light" (ibid., p. 49).

By studying the *Kabbalah* obsessively and without proper instruction and preparation to receive its mysteries, Channon became convinced that Leah was his predestined bride and that the events occurring in the outside world were a confirmation of his feelings. The more prolonged his speculations in meditation, numerology, and gematria, the greater his inwardness and the more pronounced his solitude became. When Leah's father, Sender, enters the synagogue and announces that a marriage contract has been signed and that Leah will soon be wed to Menashe, Channon falls to the ground. The messenger, who speaks at various times in riddles, allegories, and aphorisms, now intimates that a marriage may not necessarily take place even though a contract has been signed. Sender pays no heed to these mysterious prognostications. He calls for everyone to dance. When they try to awaken Channon from what they believe to be his sleep, they realize he is dead.

Act 2: The Autonomous Couple

Act 2 opens on a square in Branitz. To the left is the synagogue. Sender's house, among others, a cemetery, bridge, river, and forest are also visible. Sender is giving a feast for the poor, crippled, and old. Baskets of food are brought out and their contents devoured. The community at large is celebrating Leah's nuptials. In front and slightly to the left of the synagogue is a gravestone inscribed "Here lie a pure and holy bridegroom and bride," murdered during a pogrom as they were being led to their wedding. Not only had they been slaughtered, but half of the town's population with them. The memory of this harrowing act is still powerful within the community. After marriage ceremonies, it has been claimed, rabbis can hear sighs emanating from the grave, and so it has become the custom for all those leaving the synagogue after a wedding to dance on the tombstone in order to bring cheer to the dead couple.

Death and dance set the tone for the scene. No line is drawn between the dead buried under the earth and the living above ground: each sphere may at any moment communicate with the other. By descending into the depths of one's own being, wandering throughout the layers of this unlimited sphere, psyche and soma are one and the limits of the phenomenological world may be transcended. Traveling through the dimensions of the psyche, and in so doing examining the various soul states experienced, leads to a deepening understanding of oneself in the process of life. The mystical experience understood in this manner becomes an "instrument of self analysis, of self knowledge" (Scholem 1961, p. 341).

Dancing on the couple's tombstone and dancing with the community at large, which is expected of Leah, is also significant. As the chosen one—the bride celebrating her nuptials—Leah has taken on the stature of an archetype. She stands for youth, happiness, beauty, and spirituality (purity incarnate); she is the future bearer of children. For those whose lives are marked with despair and suffering, she radiates the positive and fruitful side of existence. Leah, the archetypal virgin, has donned her white dress and dances with the ugliest and most wretched women of the community, thereby expressing her bond with womanhood as a whole. No matter how grotesque they may be, how sordid, sullied, and repugnant their ways, each female member may dance with her youthful, harmonious soul. As they swing her round and round, touch her beautiful gown, and encircle her pliant body, polarities are unified on the earthly level.

Leah's grandmother sees that she has grown tired and tells her to stop. Leah persists, dancing with anyone and everyone who desires her. The ugliness of some of the women inspires chilled terror in her grandmother's heart. They are similar to allegorical figures representing all sorts of earthly evils. A particularly offensive creature grabs Leah and begins dancing round and round. She refuses to loosen her iron grasp, and as she twirls faster and faster, she grows hysterical. Leah turns white. Later she describes this woman's "cold, withered hands" and then faints. When consciousness returns, she feels different; something seems to have happened to her. "Someone came and lifted me from the ground and carried me far away, very far away," she informs her grandmother.

The grandmother thinks Leah is talking about "spirits" and asks her not to mention such forces. They lurk "in every tiny hole and corner and crevice," and Leah must be careful. Her spirits are not harmful nor evil, she counters. On the contrary, "it isn't evil spirits that surround us, but souls of those who died before their time and come back again to see all that we do and hear all that we say."

Just as prayer, incantation, and meditation are ways of expressing the joys of religious ecstasy, so dance is a path leading to this transcendent sphere. It is a rhythmic and ordered way of releasing emotion and bringing into being new space-time relationships that fuse with the world at large. It represents energy in a perpetual state of transformation: as captured or incorporated into an image; as an evolutive, active, dynamic concentration of forces. Every dance is a pantomime, a paradigm, a theurgic act. Plato considered the dance to be of divine origin: before becoming movement, it was sign. In biblical times, Miriam and other Hebrew women danced to express their joy after safely crossing the Red Sea; David leaped with happiness when the Ark was brought to Jerusalem. In Talmudic times, rabbis danced at weddings; in Temple times, maidens danced in the vineyards on special feast days. Hasids still express their religious enthusiasm through the dance, sometimes holding the Torah in their arms. As Leah danced, she became the incarnation of the living spirit of God, which nourishes, sustains, and energizes an entire community. The dance not only put Leah in contact with the world at large but allowed her to become emotionally attuned to the universe and thus to participate in its very fabric. It encouraged her to release her fears, pain, and joy. Through it, she created patterns in space, enacted desires and needs, and penetrated the external sphere, thereby divesting herself of her mortality. Leah experiences inner and outer worlds simultaneously: the light and the dark, life and death.

The circularity of her patterns made her grow dizzy and intoxicated her very being. Like the dervishes, Leah knew a kind of ecstasy. The circularity and speed of her dance allowed the rational sphere to lower its barriers and permitted contents from the collective unconscious to become constellated and animated. Leah grew faint because the archetypal material within her had become so powerful that an eclipse of her conscious orientation ensued. That something foreign had entered her ordered workaday world which left her disturbed and ill at ease is not surprising. Just as the volume of water increases during a spring thaw, so Leah's circular and rotating movements released those powers (instincts) that had been building within her and had previously been held in check. The dance had created a physical and psychological condition which failed to contain her archaic world. Conflicts surfaced, and by them consciousness was overwhelmed.

The image of the circle or mandala which characterizes Leah's dance is an iconographic representation of the ultimate state of oneness for both psychologists and alchemists. It is a synthesis of the four elements, a synthesis that alchemists consider the most perfect of forms; the "sun point" or the "light" and "fire" of deity. The circle symbolizes a reconciliation of opposites, as in the alchemist's hermetic vessel; the circle is the cooking pot, the womb, the chalice, the cauldron. It stands for that essential force which may eventually lead to the creation of the philosopher's stone or to mystical union with the All. The circle also stands for the psyche, the complete entity, including the suprapersonal values that, in Leah's case, have at least momentarily invaded and drowned her ego (Harding 1973, p. 323).

Dazzled and dazed by the circularity of her dance, she experiences in this vertiginous condition a release from the world of conflict (reality) and feels inundated with sensations of love and beatitude. A new soul invades her being. She explains to her grandmother the difference between evil spirits and souls who die before their lives are over, saying that young souls who have not been allowed to fulfill their destinies do not disappear. She wonders where Channon's soul is.

> What becomes of the life he has not lived, do you think? What becomes of his joys and sorrows and all the thoughts he had no time to think and all the things he hadn't time to do? No human life goes to waste. If one of us dies before his time, his soul returns to the world to complete its span, to do the things left undone and experience the happiness and griefs he would have known.

In a state of elation now, Leah will go to the cemetery and ask her mother (who died when she was still a child) to join her under the wedding canopy.

> She will be with me there, and after the ceremony we shall dance together. It is the same with all the souls who leave the world before their time. They are here in our midst, unheard and invisible. Only if your desire is strong enough, you can see them and hear their voices and learn their thoughts.

Leah tells her grandmother that the bride and groom buried in front of the synagogue have communicated with her in both dreams and waking states. She identifies with them, experiencing them both inwardly and outwardly, as psychic and material entities. There is no separation for her between the world of the living and that of the dead.

Music is heard. Menashe is approaching the square. The messenger explains the mysterious events about to occur.

> The souls of the dead *do* return to earth, but not as disembodied spirits. Some must pass through many forms before they achieve

purification . . . . The souls of the wicked return in the form of beasts, or birds, or fish . . . . They have to wait for the coming of some righteous sage to purge them of their sins and set them free. Others enter the bodies of the newly born, and cleanse themselves by well-doing.

There are vagrant souls which, finding neither rest nor harbor, pass into the bodies of the living, in the form of a dybbuk, until they have attained purity.

Sender encourages Leah to go to the graveyard and invite her mother to the wedding.

Ask her to be with you, so that we may lead our only daughter under the canopy together. Say that I have fulfilled her dying wishes to devote my life to you and bring you up to be a true and virtuous daughter of Israel.

Leah asks the grandmother if she can invite friends to her wedding, but she is told only relatives are acceptable. When she nevertheless insists on inviting Channon, the grandmother warns that because of his "unnatural death," fearsome consequences may be in the offing. He has come to her in a dream, Leah confesses. "He told me his trouble and begged me to invite him to the wedding."

The grandmother reveals that Leah, when communicating with the dead souls, had fainted. After the incident she has become a changed person. As Menashe and his family are about to come on stage, Leah suddenly tears off the veil which hides her face and screams out: "No! You are not my bridegroom!" She runs to the grave where the holy bride and groom are buried and asks them for protection. She "looks wildly about" and in a masculine voice shouts: "Ah! Ah! You have buried me. But I have come back—to my destined bride. I will leave her no more!" The messenger speaks: "Into the bride has entered a dybbuk."

She is no longer the Leah she was. A new being has taken possession of her. Psychologically, she is split. As long as she had been able to remain the virgin girl, the adolescent answerable only to her father and to the community at large, equilibrium was maintained within her psyche. In the way that Channon represented the fire principle, Leah symbolized air. She functioned well in the dreamy atmosphere of one who looks forward to marriage and motherhood at some remote time. As long as she could circulate as lightly as air, her spirit found release and contentment in her imaginary lover. No demands were made upon her on a personal level. Once responsibilities were imposed, her balance shattered. Her spirit became compressed and heat and fire mounted, burning their way through her already enfeebled ego. With the breakdown of relationships between fantasy and reality, a redistribution of values came into being with which she could not cope. The world of fantasy took over.

That Leah maintained such a close relationship with her dead mother's soul, as well as with the souls of the deceased couple, indicates that she had no individuality, no reality of her own, and that she lived a sublimated existence as an airborne principle. She took on stature only as a collective object: as her father's daughter, Channon's soul image, and the community's symbol of purity and beauty. In her white wedding dress, her amorphous personality reflected the innocence, spontaneity, and openness of one with singleness of vision. Leah could be called a medial woman. She stands at the threshold of two worlds: a bridge between the living and the dead, the real and the unreal. She reflects both the moods of the community and those of the protagonists. She thus is a moon image, unable to generate energy but reflecting it. An agent, a vessel, an intermediary, she is a conveyor of feeling and remains, therefore, embedded in the psychic atmosphere of her environment. As a carrier of the positive side of the community's psyche, she is joy, luster, balance, and health incarnate. When representing the community's shadow, she becomes a negative force, the carrier of death and destruction. Since she has no perception or objectivity of her own, she lacks the power to discriminate and is overwhelmed by the community as well as by her own collective unconscious. Leah's case is tragic because she is undeveloped and emerges from her ordeal victimized by the very forces she had hoped to serve.

While Channon's protracted experience in religious ecstasy destroyed whatever rational attitudes he had possessed, the dance, with its circular and swirling movements and ensuing vertigo, diminished Leah's conscious orientation. Once the barriers protecting her feeble ego weakened, the collective forces within her psyche flowed forth. The cemetery sequence, when Leah lost consciousness for the second time, encouraged her further to fall under the spell of nonpersonal powers or the plurality of autonomous complexes within her psyche (Jung 1960, par. 587).

There is a "rite of Leah" in *Kabbalah* which is performed by the devout at midnight. The rite symbolizes God uniting with His formerly exiled Shekinah (Scholem 1961, pp. 228–30). It is a power-fully solemn and moving celebration of mystical nuptials which enriches the believer and fills him with harmony and divine benevo-lence. It is an outward manifestation of an inner fusion in the psyche. Such a union was described by alchemists as a marriage of king and queen, a harmonious blending of metals in their purest Golden State. Mystical hymns drawn from the Song of Songs were frequently intoned by the alchemist during these sacred moments, adding to the beauty and intensity of the emotions evoked.

Leah's inner marriage, however, was not an expression of her harmony. On the contrary, it symbolized destruction: the end of any hope that she could return to the real world as a functioning being. The progressive invasion of collective forces allowed Channon, an animus image (her unconscious vision of her soul mate) to reign over every area of her existence. He had absorbed her airborne nature. Darkness invaded her world, not light; idea had become form. The image of Channon, far more powerful than an abstract concept, imposed its own logic and dimensionality onto her world. It could no longer be dissolved; it had hardened like steel. The diamond Channon had so desperately wished to create had now come into being in the birth of a new soul, a divine child fashioned out of air and fire and removed from the earthly sphere.

Channon, the fire principle, had succeeded in luring Leah away from the world of reality into his own sphere of disembodied souls. Although he possessed no objective reality, he lived on in her as a most powerful force which fascinated and mesmerized her. Leah found solace only in her subjective domain, absorbed by the fantasy figure which she found more pleasing than the patriarchal society of which she was a product. In her new land of quietude, she no longer had to envision marriage with someone she did not know. Her passion for Channon encouraged her to fall under the magic of his feeling world. Each time he calls to her, therefore, she yields to his embrace.

Act 3: Exorcism—The Transformation Ritual

Act 3 begins with the aged Rabbi Azrael Miropol, dressed in a white caftan and high fur cap, seated in his home deep in thought. Pain marks his features. He begins speaking of the Holy Land, the seventy nations, the seventy tongues referred to in the Bible, and the trans-migration of souls.

But it happens sometimes that a soul which has attained to the final state of purification suddenly becomes the prey of evil forces which cause it to slip and fall. And the higher it has soared, the deeper it falls. And with the fall of such a soul as this, a world plunges to ruin. And darkness overwhelms the spheres. The ten spheres bewail the world that it lost.

Leah's father has asked Rabbi Azrael to exorcise the dybbuk that has lodged in his daughter. He assures the rabbi that she is sinless and gentle. "She has never disobeyed," he adds.

The rabbi is plagued by doubt. Is he really capable of performing an exorcism? Is he God's deputy on earth? He longs to experience the nearness of the Almighty; his being yearns for solitude and rest. Yet, despite his age, people keep coming from far and near to his door, begging for comfort and spiritual healing. Their words pierce his flesh because he feels inadequate to the task.

There are moments when he thinks back upon his forebears, great rabbis who had helped the ill. Such thoughts strengthen him. His grandfather, for example, could drive out dybbuks through spells or incantations and with only a single word of command. Each time the rabbi talks about these men, he is infused with energy. He feels his continuity with the past. The generations of archetypal powers represented by these souls arouse energetic factors within him. Under such circumstances, time has become reversible. Like chemical substances, so powers condense, integrate, and fixate. Prayers, meditation, and his deep faith have put him in touch and in harmony with his inner world—his past—which lives within him in both a personal and collective state (von Franz 1972, p. 197).

A drastic personality change has come about in Leah. Her psyche has literally fallen apart and reorganized under two distinct, autonomous complexes. Schizophrenics have frequently alluded to voices they hear when the ego is no longer the center of consciousness. In Leah's case, the ego has been displaced by the collective unconscious. The passivity that had marked Leah's life did not permit her to act overtly once her father had prepared for her nuptials, yet she also could not pursue a course inimicable to her feelings. The only solution to the impasse was severing the link with her conscious life. Since she could not discharge strong emotion in the workaday world, she yielded to that other personality within her. The dybbuk took dominion. "I am one of those who sought other paths," Leah tells the rabbi in Channon's voice. It was not the straight Talmudic way, but the evil path of magic, theurgy, and Satan.

The rabbi commands the dybbuk to leave the world of the living. He refuses.

> I have nowhere to go. Every world is barred against me and every gate is locked. On every side, the forces of evil lie in wait to seize me. And now that my soul has found refuge from the bitterness and terror of pursuit, you wish to drive me away. Have mercy! Do not send me away—don't force me to go!

Although the rabbi pities Channon's wandering soul, he again orders him to depart. Still the dybbuk refuses. The rabbi will now have to resort to "malediction and anathema." He asks for white shrouds, seven rams' horns, seven black candles, and seven holy scrolls. He requests that the city rabbi be called to participate in the proceedings and that Menashe, who had gone to his family in the next town, should return for the wedding ceremony.

The number seven, a mystic force for both kabbalists and alchemists, is archetypal and as such is endowed with energy. For the mystic whose visions of the divine realm are to be found in Ezekiel (1:26), seven created a link between man and divinity, thus healing the schism that came into being with the Creation and later the Fall. The love principle is also inherent in the number seven, which prompted the allusion to the seven petals of a rose in the Song of Songs. A complete cycle is also represented by seven: the marriage of four (the square; earthly realm, realm of matter), with three (the pyramid, the triangle)—that is, the wedding of the complete with the incomplete, the unconscious with consciousness, gold with lead. According to the Bible, there were seven priests who blew on seven rams' horns during the battle of Jericho. The struggle resulted in victory: the known over the unknown.

Rabbi Samson from the next village arrives. He tells Rabbi Azrael of a dream he had had the previous night: Nissin ben Rifke, a young Hasid who used to come to town twenty years earlier, appeared to him three times and demanded that Leah's father be summoned before the rabbinical court, the highest religious tribunal. Rabbi Samson's dream was revelatory. Such dreams occur when the dreamer experiences a feeling of oneness with the universe. He no longer feels like a separate being, but rather as if he belongs to a fourth dimension, where past, present, and future no longer exist in a linear time scheme but reveal themselves under certain circumstances in forms and images. The fourth dimension may be regarded as Janus-faced, pointing back to a preconscious prehistoric world of instincts while at the same time it potentially anticipates a future (Jung 1960, par. 493). Because Rabbi Samson's ego is so well grounded, his three visions, rather than overwhelming him, enlarge his frame of reference, activate his will, and integrate his thoughts, enabling him to deal most effectively with the problem confronting him. His dream indicated that some important act of deception that had led to a crucial misunderstanding had to be brought out into the open. Although stunned by Rabbi Samson's revelations, Sender agrees to be called before the court.

Act 4: The Spagyric Marriage

In act 4, the rabbinical court comes into session and the interrogation begins. Rabbi Azrael calls Nissin ben Rifke to be present at the trial. He then draws a circle counterclockwise, beyond which the dead soul may not pass. He asks Michael, the attendant, to take his staff and go to the cemetery. He must knock three times on the first grave and then ask (three times) for the dead to forgive him for disturbing their peace. He must further request that Nissin ben Rifke be present at the trial. When returning, he must never once look back, no matter how painful the cries or shrieks he may hear. To do so is to invite dire consequences.

In mystical and theurgic practices, the circle represents a protected area where evil may never enter. The same precautions doctors take against the spread of infection are taken by exorcists when driving out tainted or contaminated souls. Under such conditions, rituals are of utmost importance. For the mystic, evil is purified; for the psychologist, the ego remains clear and cleansed (Harding 1971, p. 59).

The circle or mandala isolates the personal from the collective psyche. Foreign influences or disparate psychic elements under the domination of other centers are replaced when encircled by the partial rulership of the ego, thereby giving weight and balance to the entire psyche. Since circles protect and delimit, it is believed that alien spirits are unable to cross the line. Psychologically, this belief implies that when an individual is concerned with unknown factors, whether these be spiritual, scientific, or psychological, danger always lies in wait. What remains within the circle, alchemically, are all those elements connected with the actual experiments. They are contained within the hermetic vessel as if within the womb; they are protected and encouraged to grow. It is within the circle that fundamental transformation occurs: an idea cooks and foments, feelings incubate, metals alter, and insolubles become soluble. Alchemists go through seven processes which are repeated many times before the final phase of their Great Work comes into being. That the circle is drawn from left to right indicates that the left, associated with the unconscious, is a darkened, sinister realm where heart and emotions prevail and will be contained within boundaries. They will, however, be given the freedom to exert their influence in the rational (right) or daylight sphere.

That Michael must not look back symbolizes man submitting to law, to God, to a moral consciousness that deepens through restraint. Containment is of prime importance. If allowed to circulate freely, energy may be dispersed and the strength needed to persevere in the sacred ritual of exorcism would vanish. Interdicts have both positive and negative values: they add structure to the will; they also repress, firing up those contents within and thereby increasing their power for good or for evil. The staff or stick that Michael must take with him represents the world of celestial axis. It is comparable to the various steps in a process: it guides, points the way, and is at the same time a sign of authority. Staff symbolism plays a large role in mystical literature and myths in general. It is a means of connecting the material and nonmaterial worlds. The magic staff of the pilgrim or warrior represents authority and sovereignty. Moses' stick, when used to prove God's immanence and omniscience, was transformed into a serpent (Exodus 7:8–12). Alchemists look upon the stick as a means of altering consistencies and stages in their expriments, thereby bringing man's soul into the manifest world.

Before the trial commences, a sheet is drawn across the left-hand corner of the stage. The soul of Nissin ben Rifke will remain in front of it during the proceedings. As the circle represents a screen or partition separating the living from the dead, so the sheet enables the two worlds to communicate and yet remain protected from each other. Rabbi Samson will hear and translate Nissin ben Rifke's solemn statements. Alchemists frequently used metals as media through and by which they conducted their experiments. Rabbi Samson is also a medium. Mercury was the "medium of conjunction" and was regarded by alchemists as a kind of soul figure, a link between body and spirit (Jung 1963, par. 658).

Rabbi Samson explains the background: when Nissin ben Rifke and Sender were young, they had been best friends. They married on the same day and made a solemn vow that if one should father a boy and the other a girl, the two children would marry. Nissin ben Rifke had a son, Channon, who was "blessed with a noble and lofty soul and was progressing upwards from plane to plane." Shortly after Nissin ben Rifke's death, his son began to wander in search of "the soul to which his soul had been predestined." Finally he came to this city and while studying at the yeshivah was invited to eat his meals at Sender's table. It was there that he saw Leah and knew she was his predestined soulmate. Sender, however, was rich, and he was poor. He understood that a marriage between the two was unthinkable, since Sender was looking for a wealthy husband for his daughter. Channon grew desperate and this time, rather than taking to the provinces, he strayed spiritually from the straight paths into forbidden "New Paths." When Nissin ben Rifke realized the dangers awaiting his son, he was struck with terror. He feared those "dark powers" and their hold upon his son's soul. His fears were justified. When his son died, his soul was "severed" from "both worlds." Since neither heir nor friend remained on earth to pray or hide his soul, he was left without name or memorial. "His light has been extinguished forever."

Sender listens to the testimony and sobs. He begs forgiveness for his sin, which was committed without malice. He was unaware that the lad boarding at his home was Nissin ben Rifke's son. He should have asked his name, the court replied. Never was a question put to Channon by any member of the family. The guilt of pride, of material acquisitiveness, must be punished. The court orders Sender to give half of his fortune to the poor each year for the remainder of his days and to light a memorial candle for Nissin ben Rifke and his son and pray for their souls. It also asks Nissin ben Rifke to forgive Sender and asks the dybbuk to leave Leah's body. Sender acquiesces. Nissin ben Rifke's soul is asked to return to its resting place and in so doing not to harm any living being. The sheet is withdrawn. Rabbi Azrael traces another circle in the same area, but this time from right to left, allowing the real world to prevail instead of the unconscious or spiritual sphere. All those who participated in the calling back of a dead soul must be cleansed and purified, both physically and spiritually, and basins of water are brought in for all to wash their hands.

Despite the precautions, fear invades the atmosphere. Nissin ben Rifke has not forgiven Sender. Leah is asked to enter. She is wearing her white wedding dress and a black cloak. Rabbi Azrael commands the dybbuk to leave Leah's body. He refuses. The rabbi resorts to anathema. The seven scrolls are brought out; seven rams' horns are blown, sounding *Tekiah! Shevarim! Teruah!* The ram's horn (*shofar*) is traditionally sounded on ceremonial occasions, usually at the close of the Day of Atonement (Numbers 29:1). Since the notes are to be played in broken sounds, they resemble sobbing (*shevarim*) and wailing (*teruah*). On the other hand, *tekiah*, sounded in long, unbroken tonalities, proclaims God's sovereignty and the return of all exiles to Israel. Important, too, is the symbol of the ram's horn: it denotes the sacrifice of Isaac, when God took mercy on Abraham's son and substituted a ram for him.

During the proceedings, Leah struggles violently in her seat, as though she were being assailed by unknown and terrifying forces. The dybbuk's voice emerges from her again.

> The powers of all the world are arrayed against me. Spirits of terror wrench me and tear me without mercy—the soul of the great and righteous too have arisen against me. The soul of my own father is with them—commanding me to go—But until the last spark of strength has gone from me, so long shall I withstand them and remain where I am.

Rabbi Azrael asks that a black curtain be hung over the altar, that black candles be lit following the anathema, and that "these words rend asunder every cord that binds you to the world of the living creatures and to the body and soul of the maiden, Leah."

Black and white are both positive and negative colors; each is either a composite of all colors or divested of all color. They represent duality, opposition, conflict: black magic striking out at white magic, evil against good. Similar to the *nigredo* condition, which represents the germinal stage of the alchemical process, so blackness symbolizes the shadow, those negative and unredeemed forces at work within the personality. Unknown and uncontrollable, they inspire fear and trembling. Connected with primal forms, the unregenerate instincts working in darkness—like carbon prior to its crystallization in the diamond or dark earth in which the seed is planted—represent all that is unclean, nocturnal, unworldly; all that which has not as yet or cannot become consciously known. White, on the other hand, stands for illumination and purification of spirit, the *albedo* condition. It symbolizes the celestial spheres where air where air circulates freely and the privileged forces reside. Yet white, like lunar light, absorbs other luminescent forces and thus leads to absence and isolation. Similar to the color of dawn, white inspires a sense of futurity and may be looked upon as a new beginning, rich in potential, able to act on the soul in a clear and ordered manner, as does the day or the light of consciousness.

The messenger announces the success of the exorcism ritual. "The last spark has been swallowed up in the flame" and Channon's voice is no longer to be heard. His soul has receded. Leah's consciousness is reborn. The alchemical process has been completed. The soul has been gathered into its rightful place. The anathanor, once heated, has been cooled and the chemicals reduced to their proper proportions. The condition has been corrected.

Now that the dybbuk has departed, Rabbi Azrael lifts the ban of anathema on Channon. The black curtains and other objects used in the ritual are removed. A prayer for the dead is intoned. Everyone will leave to greet Menashe and his family, who are waiting in town. Before departing, Rabbi Azrael traces a circle around Leah, from left to right. She is not to cross the line, he warns. She still needs protection from outer forces. Leah and the grandmother remain alone.

Exhausted after her ordeal, Leah drops onto the sofa. She feels strange, a bit fearful. The grandmother assures her that no power can hurt her if she stays within the circle. If the magic circle is broken, however, spirits from the outer world may intrude, and because Leah is unprepared to deal with them, they could possess her once again. The grandmother falls asleep. Leah sighs deeply and closes her eyes. She awakens with a start. She hears Channon's voice but cannot see him. Enthralled by its tenderness, musicality, and hypnotic qualities, she tells him, "Your voice is as sweet as the lament of violins in the quiet night." She describes the beauty of her love in an emotional and lyrical passage.

I remember—your hair, so soft and damp as if with tears—your sad and gentle eyes—your hands with the thin tapering fingers. Waking and sleeping I had no thought but of you. You went away and darkness fell upon me—my soul withered in loneliness like the soul of a widow left desolate—the stranger came—and then—you returned, and the dead heart wakened to life again, and out of sorrow joy blossomed like a flower. . . . Why have you once again forsaken me?

Resplendent in her wedding dress, Leah speaks in a half-waking, half-sleeping state, as though experiencing a hypnagogic dream. Frequently such emanations emerge in mentally disturbed people when excitation or inner contents erupt into the conscious mind. The divided psyche acts as two independent forces, unconscious and autonomous. Leah views Channon as a projection; for her this psychic reality is true reality. She once again becomes the victim of an illusion. Only in such a condition could she speak words of love in such an uninhibited lyrical flow.

Channon replies.

I broke down the barriers between us—I crossed the plain of death—I defied every law of past and present time and all the ages. I strove against those who know no mercy. And as my last spark of strength left me, I left your body to return to your soul.

Leah longs for union with Channon, her soul image, for the *coniunctio* that will restore her to wholeness again.

Come back to me, my bridegroom—my husband—I will carry you, dead, in my heart—and in our dreams at night we shall rock to sleep our little children who will never be born.

The tones of the wedding march are heard. For Leah to marry anyone but Channon is now impossible. Leah entreats her true bridegroom to come to her, to make himself visible. Channon appears against the wall, wearing white robes. Although the exorcism has forced him to leave her body, he now lives more powerfully in her soul. With joy in her heart, Leah slips out of the magic circle, lured into her lover's world beyond physical reality, there to be bound to her fantasy forever. The two blend into one. "A great light flows about me," she says lovingly. "Predestined bridegroom, I am united to you forever."

The rabbi returns with the congregation and the bridegroom, but it is too late. The stage grows dark. Voices intone the same verses heard at the beginning of the drama.

Leah and Channon, the autonomous couple, live in a celestial *coniunctio*; they have undergone a spagyric marriage, a union of opposites. For the kabbalist, such a union represents superior love—a spiritual rather than a temporal relationship. For the psychologist, it is tantamount to a rejection of life or a living death. Whatever the interpretation, Leah and Channon exist in a sphere where a different modality reigns. Their psychic suffering and passion have led to a transfiguration, a kind of apotheosis. Moreover, their spagyric marriage has produced a new psychological or spiritual orientation. No longer hidden in darkness, but recognized in the world of reality, the loss which their passing represented to the community gave birth to a new principle. Leah, in the form of an anima figure, was brought into light—that is, into consciousness—and was able to assume her rightful place beside her husband. The new unity is not the product of a one-sided patriarchal society. The marriage of alchemical king and queen placed male and female on equal footing.

Channon and Leah are carriers of a mystery. Both, therefore, are relegated to the land of the deceased: the world of shades or ashes. For the alchemist, the latter is the purest of all essences. Once the residue of life has burned away, there remains only the immaculate force—the perfect diamond—which links man and woman in prismatic and flowing light.

Bibliography

Ansky, S. 1971. *The Dybbuk*. Translated by H. G. Alsberg and W. Kazin. New York: Liveright.

Artaud, A. 1958. *The Theatre and Its Double*. Translated by C. Richards. New York: Grove Press.

Epstein, P. 1978. *Kabbalah: The Way of the Jewish Mystic*. New York: Doubleday and Company.

Harding, E. 1971. *Woman's Mysteries*. New York: G. P. Putnam's Sons.

———. 1973. *Psychic Energy*. Princeton, N.J.: Princeton University Press.

Jung, C. G. 1963. *Mysterium Coniunctionis*. *CW*, vol. 14. Translated by R. F. C. Hull. Princeton, N.J.: Princeton University Press, 1970

———. 1960. *The Structure and Dynamics of the Psyche*. *CW*, vol. 8. Princeton, N.J.: Princeton University Press, 1969.

Kohansky, M. 1969. *The Hebrew Theatre: Its Fifty Years*. Jerusalem: Israel University Press.

Scholem, G. 1961. *Major Trends in Jewish Mysticism*. New York: Schocken Books.

———. 1973. *Kabbalah and Its Symbolism*. New York: Schocken Books.

———. 1971. *The Messianic Idea in Judaism*. New York: Shocken Books.

———. 1975. *Sabbatai Sevi*. Princeton, N.J.: Princeton University Press.

Stillman, J. M. 1924. *Story of Alchemy and Early Chemistry*. New York: Dover Publications, 1960.

von Franz, M.-L. 1972. *Creation Myths*. Zurich: Spring Publications.

———. 1974. *Number and Time*. Translated by A. Dykes. Evanston, Ill.: Northwestern University Press.

Rabbi Nachman's "The Loss
of the Princess"

The Shekinah/Anima's Exile
and Restoration

"The Loss of the Princess," by the Hasidic Rabbi Ben Simhah Nachman of Bratslav (1772–1810), is a homiletic tale. While its plot is simple, its mystical and psychological ramifications are vast. Like a palimpsest, it may be understood on multiple levels, depending on the depth of the reader's projection.

"The Loss of the Princess" is about a king who has six sons but only one daughter, his most beloved. One day, he unexpectedly bursts out against her in anger: "May the Not-Good take you away." The daughter retires to her room; the following morning she is gone. Deeply grieved by her departure, the king sends out search parties but all efforts to find her are unsuccessful. The viceroy, understanding the king's profound sense of bereavement, sets out to find the princess. After many years of wandering and concerted efforts to overcome superhuman ordeals, he finally succeeds in restoring the princess to the king.

When viewed as a religious discourse, a kind of allegorical sermon or informal exposition of scriptures, the characters and events imbricated in "The Loss of the Princess" convey a spiritual as well as a psychological message. The "loss" felt by the king after the princess's departure, for example, suggests a theory concerning God's creation of the world that is at variance with the one depicted in Genesis. As enunciated by the Jerusalem-born kabbalist, Isaac Luria (1534–1572), the coming into being of the world resulted from a withdrawal of the Godhead into Himself rather than an expansion of His powers into space (to be discussed later). Psychologically, such an inner flow of energy replicates the human condition of introversion instead of the extroversion implied in the outward flow of libido (psychic energy) depicted in Genesis.

In keeping with the kabbalistic diagram of the Sefiroth, an image of God's Ten Emanations into the empirical domain, the king in Nachman's tale becomes a paradigm for Divinity (see chart of the Sefiroth). As Kether, or the Crown, he represents the highest and uncognizable all-inclusive Sefiroth. In psychological terms, the king symbolizes the Self (or total psyche). When the tale begins, the Godhead is seemingly unable to deal with the sudden outbreak of sparring components within His psyche. The same may be said on a human level of a usually harmonious individual who stumbles on an emotional situation that he or she cannot handle. The princess and the viceroy may also be considered analogical aspects of the Sefiroth, both being active aspects of Divinity. She, as the Shekinah, a manifestation of the community of Israel as well as the feminine element within God Himself, may be viewed psychologically as soul or as anima (man's unconscious feminine side). Generally, a well-tempered condition prevailed within the king's personality. When the princess was hurt by the imbalance between the king/Kether/Self's rash, unthinking, and flamboyant ego (center of consciousness), she left the palace and the kingdom. Her departure created a vacuum that changed the status quo. The lack of interconnectedness that had led to the king/Kether/Self's inability to deal with His princess/Shekhinah/anima required a psychological dismemberment or dissolution of the whole. The exile of the princess/Shekhinah/anima and the strong affect the king/Kether/Self experienced serves in part to reshuffle subliminal components. The viceroy—the king's envoy, therefore, an aspect of the king/Kether/Self—in keeping with the Sefirotic chart may be identified with Hokhmah, the "wisdom" of the primordial idea of God. Psychologically, the viceroy represents the courageous and well-meaning but not always wise and disciplined ego setting out on its quest to restore what has been lost. The concentration and inner reserves needed to overcome multiple ordeals and the energy expended during the viceroy's search process activate his subliminal contents. As a projection of the king/Kether/Self, the reshuffling of the viceroy's libido alters the climate within the Sefiroth, the former condition of imbalance—created by the outpouring of negative affects—yielding to one of harmony. With the reintegration of what had been

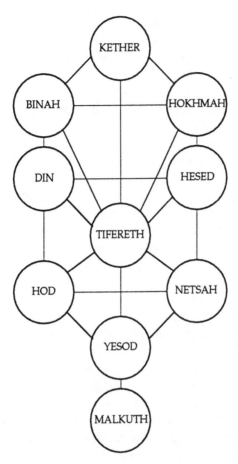

lost and shattered, cohesion is restored to the Sefiroth, fostering formerly prevailing qualities of compassion, love, and caring.

A lesson then may be gleaned by the reader of "The Loss of the Princess." The manner in which the author traces a spiritual development in his tale by fragmenting the One, Deity or Self, into the Two, princess (anima) and viceroy (ego), not only takes on numinosity but also becomes a blueprint for individuals in their quest for individuation.

Although Rabbi Nachman was the great-grandson of the Baal Shem Tov ("The Master of the Good Name") and was born in his master's native city, Medzhibozh, he differed from him. Unlike the founder of the new brand of Hasidism, he was unable to experience God in joy. Deeply tormented as an adolescent and youth, Nachman often fasted and spent sleepless nights hoping and praying that by engaging in such ascetic practices, he would know the *ekstasis* of the Divine presence. Nachman's existence revolved around his search for God. So deeply in need of transcending earthly involvements, he not only related poorly to people but found himself nonfunctional in the workaday world. Linear time and routines were simply beyond his ken. Nor did he find peace when performing community service, an obligation expected of every Jew in the community. Habitually, rather than return home at night, he retreated to some secluded space in town and there spoke to God. Because Nachman felt his prayers had gone unanswered, he despairingly concluded that Divinity had not made his presence known to him. His yearning to serve God reached such extremes that at night he withdrew to the cemetery to pray at the grave of the Baal Shem Tov. One day, in the depths of anguish, he was overwhelmed by the "first shudder of rapture" (Buber 1956, p. 22). He knew then that he had experienced a visitation. Thereafter, his life changed dramatically.

According to custom, Nachman married at fourteen and moved to his father-in-law's house in Usyatin, in the eastern part of the Ukraine. Having lived a citified ghetto existence until this time, he had never been exposed to nature. In his new countrified environment, he experienced a powerful sense of exaltation as he looked upon the sheer beauty of trees, plants, forests, ponds, rivers, and mountains. Some mysterious inner force seemed to have flooded his being. Not only did he feel his soul breathing freely as never before, but he also began to experience the meaning of love in God's presence within him. Nachman wrote:

> When man becomes worthy to hear the songs of the plants, how each plant speaks its song to God, how beautiful and sweet it is to hear their singing! And, therefore, it is good indeed to serve God in their midst in solitary wandering over the fields between the growing things and to pour out one's speech before God in truthfulness. All the speech of the fields enters then into your own and intensifies its strength. With every breath you drink in the air of paradise, and when you return home, the world is renewed in your eyes. (Ibid., p. 24)

Nachman also came to realize at this juncture in his life that books alone were incapable of helping him to impart the new emotions of joy and love he now felt in his heart. Nor could a strictly cerebral approach be efficacious in helping him to communicate with his fellow beings. No longer would he isolate himself: more like the Baal Shem Tov, he would live with and relate to people, sharing in their joys and helping to heal their wounds. He would become a teacher. Before setting out on his new profession, however, he felt a deep need to visit and immerse himself in the Holy Land. Only there, he was convinced, would he be able to bathe in that ecstasy he needed for renewal. By praying in the Holy Land at the graves of two renowned Hebrew kabbalists, Simeon bar Yohai and Isaac Luria, he would succeed, psychologically speaking, in connecting with an ancient past. Simeon bar Yohai (2nd century C.E.) was a visionary whose doctrines were believed to have been incorporated into the kabbalistic work known as the *Zohar* ("The Book of Splendor"). Isaac Luria, referred to as Ari (the "holy lion"), was the founder of an extraordinary school of Jewish mysticism that became the basis for later Hasidic thought.

Rabbi Nachman left for the Holy Land in 1798. Extremely poor, he sold his furniture to pay for his trip and placed his wife and children in the care of strangers in the Ukraine. Although he had to contend with both political and financial difficulties, he succeeded in setting foot in the Holy Land. His sojourn took on apocalyptic proportions for him, imbuing him with the deepest sense of beatitude. The Holy Land represented the embodiment of the mystical Shekinah, the very "indwelling" of Divinity Himself (Buber 1956, p. 27).

Upon his return to Russia, Rabbi Nachman settled in Bratislava. Because his ideas appealed to only a minority in the community, he made many enemies. Nevertheless, hate having been banished from his heart, he looked upon even those who castigated him as good people. As a teacher, his ability to communicate with his disciples brought him fulfillment in a continuously evolving and wonderful creation which he described as follows:

> The word moves a bit of air, and this the next, until it reaches the man who receives the word of his friend and receives his soul therein and is therein awakened. (Ibid., p. 29)

Nevertheless, his years of fasting and poverty had taken their physical toll on Nachman. Succumbing to tuberculosis, he faced death not with fear but with love. It would enable him to ascend, he thought, to a higher plane of being and to dwell with Divinity. He made but one request of his disciples: to bring him to the town of Uman to die. Why Uman? Because the entire Jewish population had been slaughtered there in 1768. Since Nachman believed in Isaac Luria's doctrine that if souls die before their time they are bound to the place where their life ended and cannot ascend to heaven until another soul helps them to do so, he wanted his soul to assist in the realization of this act. That the window of the house he occupied in Uman gave onto "the house of life," as the Jewish cemetery was called, allowed him to fulfill his wish and there he died in peace.

The Lurianic Approach to Creation

The king's despair in "The Loss of the Princess" and his withdrawal into himself after the disappearance of his daughter may be viewed as an empirical replica of Isaac Luria's kabbalistic concept of Creation.

Luria's cosmogonical system is all the more astonishing and fascinating—and certainly innovative—because of the difficulty one has in imagining a condition of profound introversion and despair as conducive to creativity. And yet, according to Luria, it was God's exile or withdrawal into Himself that catalyzed the bringing of the world into existence. Traditional theologians approach the cosmic drama of Creation as a *creatio ex nihilo* ("creation out of nothingness")—an externalization, unfolding, projection, or outflowing of God's divine energy from Himself into space. According to Luria's credo, God's act of withdrawal, contraction, or concentration into Himself—his essence becoming increasingly hidden in the process—led to the liberation of primordial or pneumatic space, from which the manifest world came into being (Scholem 1973, p. 110).

For Luria and his disciples, Divinity's exile into Himself, which he called *tsimtsum*, was a theological answer to the Jews' historical experiences of the "catastrophe": their expulsion from what they considered to be their native land at the time. One of the most significant took place during the Inquisition and the forced ejection of the Jews from Spain in 1492. Their flight—the alternatives were either burning at the stake or conversion to Catholicism—was looked upon by Luria as a paradigm of a soul in exile. The association made between God's exile within Himself and the suffering of the displaced Spanish Jews, indeed, of all exiles from earliest times to the present day, is also applicable to a sorrow that triggers a condition of introversion. The inflow of libido in such cases serves to activate the creative process.

Parallels between Divinity's theogonic process, as in *tsimtsum*, and the human act of creation are also in order. It may be suggested that just as Divinity relinquished a space within Himself through an inner movement, thus making room for the "mystical primordial space" to come into being, He also paved the way for the return of his essence in less concentrated form in his Creation. Likewise the writer, or any creative individual, may make his or her work accessible to others through a retreat into his or her infinite and boundless collective unconscious (Scholem 1965, p. 261). Nachman's periods of indwelling in the Holy Land as well as in his youth had, for example, energized his subliminal spheres in like manner, allowing him to create his homiletic tale. A similar psychological vigor could be said to have been operational when the Renaissance Platonist Marsilio Ficino (1433–1499) composed such seminal works as his *Book of Life*.

The concept of *tsimtsum*, or internalization in human terms, cuts the creative individual off from the everyday world while also drawing him into his or her own undifferentiated inner dominion. During the writer's, artist's, composer's, or scientist's period of withdrawal, tension is aroused in the subliminal sphere by the inflow of libido, which had been previously expended dealing with external matters. The nebulous idea, feeling, image, or sensation with which the artist had been wrestling prior to his or her retreat may now—like the seed planted in the dark, moist, and fertile earth—be nurtured by the activated nutrients existing inchoate within the individual's subliminal spheres. It is in such a region that gestation occurs.

During periods of intense creativity many writers (e.g., Proust, Emily Brontë, Dickinson) knowingly exiled themselves from the workaday world in order better to channel and concentrate their energies on a particular project. To retreat into the transpersonal inner recesses of the psyche is to penetrate a world generally inaccessible to conscious understanding. This collective unconscious or suprapersonal, undifferentiated, and nonindividual inner ocean, regarded as the deepest layer within the subliminal world, may act as an enriching force for the artist. The incipient archetypal images living within its depths may, under certain circumstances, emerge in concrete form, as symbolic representations of inner contents seeking expression.

Religions, myths, and legends were and are born from this primordial inner space, as are eternal and universal works of art. It is from these subliminal layers that great writers draw their material and that the king in "The Loss of the Princess" renewed and restored harmony within his own Divine Kingdom. The same process may be said to be operational on an earthly and human realm.

The Sefiroth as God's Ten Emanations

Because the Sefiroth, symbolizing for the kabbalist God's Ten Emanations, cannot be perceived directly by the mind, it is considered to be unknowable. As such, it has been identified as aspects of the hidden Divinity (*En-Sof*). The Sefiroth, represented frequently in the image of the Tree of God, stands for the deepest layers of mystical consciousness. It is within each Sefirah (singular of Sefiroth) that God exists in his infinitude and hiddenness as well as in His finitude. The Ten Emanations, as perceived by kabbalists, allow the faithful to experience His attributes both in the differentiated sphere and in the world of the absolute. In the latter happening, the qualities of the Sefiroth are sensed; in the former, they are expressed qualitatively and hierarchically.

The highest Sefiroth, encompassing all of Divinity's qualities—His divine energy, His divine light, His divine language—is referrred to as the "crown of the holy king" or the "supreme crown" of God: Kether Elyon. As the crowning or supernal emblem of Divinity, it becomes a metaphor for "the king's faces," or Divinity's multiple yet single aspects. Because Kether stands for an unmanifested force—an unfathomed aspect within the Godhead and, by extension, of the human personality—it may be viewed, psychologically, as the Self. In that the crown is usually placed on a head, it is associated with the highest form or preeminence of consciousness. Because it is made of gold, the crown shoots out its beams or scintillae of light in dazzling arrays, catalyzing the advent of spiritual and psychological energetic patterns. As such, the crown or Kether may be said to function as a mediating force between celestial and earthly spheres. In that Kether is identified with the *En-Sof* (the hidden God or "hidden Root of all Roots"), it remains incomprehensible to mortals except to the most evolved, and even to them, only in glimpses or in sparks of light emanating from it. What fragments may be fathomable to the mystic on an occult plane and to the ordinary person on a psychological level may trigger flamboyant and flamelike feelings and thoughts in the individual undergoing the numinous experience.

Because Kether, or the crown, represents God, it stands for the world of the absolute: invisible, transcendent, circular, and eternal. In that its visible or finite form may be apprehended in the empirical world, it unites spiritual and human domains. Likewise the ego reveals itself in an individual's comportment, while the Self activates what exists in a potential state within an individual's psyche.

The King as Self

The king/Kether complex in Nachman's mystical tale, then, may be identified, psychologically, with the Self. In the Divine hierarchy, Kether, as previously mentioned, is the highest, most remote, and infinite manifestation of Divinity. Because the entire Sefiroth, as well as each of its Ten Emanations, are archetypes (representative of aspects of Divinity's psychic energy, both individually and collectively), they act and react upon each other. Interaction is continuous: everything that one or more of God's attributes symbolizes reflects upon the other nine Sefiroth. Anything that happens to or any action taken by the king/Kether/Self impacts on one and all of His other aspects.

Let us glance briefly at the other nine hierarchized forms of the Sefiroth: Hokhmah (the "wisdom" of the primordial idea of God); Binah (the "intelligence" of God); Hesed (the "love," "grace," or "mercy" of God); Gevurah or Din (the "power" of God, chiefly manifested as the power of stern judgment and punishment); Tifereth ("beauty," love, the heart and "compassion" of God); Netsah (the "lasting endurance" of God); Hod (the "majesty" of God); Yesod (the "basis" or "foundation" of God); Malkuth or Shekinah (the "kingdom" of God, or Israel's mystical community, or "a quasi-independent feminine element within Him") (Scholem 1965, p. 213). Since each of the Ten Emanations arouses not only itself but also everything else within the complex, if disruption occurs—be it between active and passive elements, masculine and feminine forces, or constraints and expansions within the whole— inner balance is disturbed. When the Sefiroth works in harmony with its components, balance prevails: God is connected with Himself and, therefore, with all of His attributes—His source of being. Because of His inner and outer connectedness, He is empowered to revive what has withered and restore to life what has died. The psyche functions similarly, in accordance with its own mysterious conscious or unconscious laws.

The king, as a symbol of Kether/Self, is a transpersonal figure and energetic principle. Within him are incorporated infinite abstract qualities that become manifest in their finite forms as personality traits. As Kether/Self, the king occupies the primary place in Nachman's tale, symbolizing the One as well as the multiple, the absolute and the empirical counterpart. Psychologically, he may be said to exist as pre- and post-thought, pre- and post-reality: abstractly in the mind, prior to manifestation, thereby inaccessible, unknowable, and invisible to human understanding.

As a paradigm of the infinite or hidden God, the king in Nachman's tale is a nonhuman protagonist who lives in a nonhuman environment. The reader is told nothing about the king. We know only that he has six sons and that his only daughter "was extremely important to him and he cherished her and enjoyed her company very much." Nor do we know why on a specific day "he became enraged at her and from his mouth slipped the sentence: 'May the Not-Good take you away.' "

The loss of the princess as the Shekinah, or Divinity's last Emanation (the lowest in the hierarchy, thereby closest to the empirical sphere, and thus more accessible to human understanding), suggests, on a psychological level, the exile of love and relatedness within the Godhead. The severing of this archetypal attribute (anima) causes king/Kether/Self extreme despair. Alienation, agitation, and grief set in. For the kabbalist, the Shekinah's exile symbolizes that the king is severed from part of Himself, or that "a part of God Himself is exiled from God" (Scholem 1973, p. 107).

Although we are not told what devastating incident provoked the king's outburst, we do know that he was unable to cope with the emotional stress it caused. Anger soon turned to excoriating grief. On a psychological level, we may infer that the king had allowed his unthinking or irrational side to flare up destructively and hurtfully. We may suggest, in analogy with the Sefiroth, that Divinity's uncontrollable Gevurah, or "stern judgment" attribute, had exploded. The intensity of His affect had displaced or unsettled God's—or, in Nachman's tale, the king's—former radiance. Various responses are available to the king: either he does not act, thereby allowing pain and a condition of dissociation to prevail, or he accepts and lives through his anguish, thus paving the way for a new arrangement of unconscious contents to flow into consciousness. By choosing the latter solution, the king, rectifying a distorted condition in his personality, would make his creative side operational.

The anger episode, interpreted as an externalization of an unsatisfactory inner condition within the Godhead or, psychologically, the Self, has brought to an end the accustomed order of things. So powerful was the confusion and turbulence of the affect that the princess/Shekinah/anima, one of the archetypal roots, exiled herself, thereby bringing about a vacuum in the king/Kether/ Self complex. The emptiness of chaos prevails. His inability to communicate or to bind with the eros factor in Him, represented by the anima, indicates that that part of his personality that accounted for His lovable qualities has vanished.

The Princess/Shekinah/Anima

How may we define the complex and enigmatic term of Shekinah? One of the Ten Manifestations of God in the Sefiroth, the Shekinah was first alluded to in the *Book of Bahir* (12th century) and later, in the thirteenth-century kabbalistic work, the *Zohar*. For some mystics, the Shekinah, as suggested above, symbolizes the feminine element within the Godhead and/or the mystical body of the community of Israel. In the human domain, it may be identified with the feminine principle and/or the soul/anima. When the princess/ Shekinah/anima is said to be in exile, she is cut off from God, humankind, and herself, thus from the whole. Understandably, her suffering is intense. When she is united with God, joy and harmony prevail (Scholem 1973, p. 107).

Because communion between God and His creation is so close, whenever He is separated from any part of Himself—in this case, his Shekinah—His torment and suffering is said to be mirrored in each of the Sefiroth. When such a cleavage takes place on terrestrial or celestial planes, the Shekinah weeps in anguish: she "tastes the other, bitter side, and then her face is dark." The abandonment the Shekinah experiences as a result of her exile from God or, on a human level, during periods of individual and collective banishments, wanderings, or persecution of Jews, may leave her to wither from neglect or even die from lack of nourishment. Severed from God or the Tree of Life, she is transformed into the "Tree of Death." When working in harmony with Divinity, she becomes a positive, protective, and nourishing power. It is she, according to kabbalists, who guided the exiled Jacob, also named Israel (Genesis 32:29), and his people to their rightful destination. The Shekinah's enforced separation may also be said to effect a rekindling and rechanneling of her power in the earthly sphere, thereby helping to reroot and enrich those in need.

God and His Shekinah are consubstantial. Thus the Shekinah, or "a part of God [His anima] is exiled from God" may be interpreted psychologically as a projection of a harrowing drama occurring within a human personality. The banishment of the unconscious, feminine side of a masculine personality implies a one-sided emotional condition in the individual or in the collective (a nation). The alienation of the anima—that soul force or relational (eros) factor with which the Shekinah is frequently identified—creates a vacuum and a sense of loss or bereavement sometimes leading to dissociation within the psyche. Instead of encouraging awareness and fomenting the healing process, the inner void may tear mind and heart asunder. Redemption or restoration of the anima to the whole personality is viewed in the mystical realm as the reuniting of Divinity with His Shekinah. At this juncture, it may be posited that masculine and feminine powers flow smoothly and unimpeded throughout the Godhead, linking earthly and celestial spheres. The same condition of interconnectedness may be said to exist in terms of the components of the human personality. With the restoration of unity, chaos is transformed into cosmos.

In the *Zohar*, the Shekinah appears as Queen, Daughter, and Bride of Divinity, as well as universal Mother. Because of her many guises in the *Zohar*, she has come to be referred to as a symbol of "eternal womanhood" (Scholem 1965, p. 230). When alluded to as the Daughter, she symbolizes the lower feminine principle in the Sefiroth. When identified as Mother or Queen, she represents Tifereth, or the higher or more remote feminine principle. Because of her ability to radiate the appropriate hierarchized factor, she can communicate even more meaningfully and in the closest of ways with humankind. It is she, then, who may enter the empirical world with ease; it is she who sheds her scintillae, or fragments of that infinite blinding Divine light inhabiting the entire Sefiroth, thereby actively redeeming what has been degraded. Quoting the kabbalist Isaac Luria, Scholem writes: " 'Sparks of the Shekinah' are scattered in all worlds and there is no sphere of existence including organic and inorganic nature that is not full of holy sparks" (Scholem 1965, p. 280).

That the princess, a symbol of the Shekinah/anima, vanished from the king's castle after having been verbally maligned and/or chastised, is understandable in view of the patriarchal dominant operating in Nachman's tale. Neither eros nor the feeling world of the heart is operational in the king's world. As an anima figure, the princess feels hurt. Ashamed, she hides her pain. Time, essential to the healing of a wound, allows the meditative process to function. The pull and tug of her distress will activate other Sefiroth within the king/Kether/Self complex. New channels may be opened, paving the way for a freer-flowing libido and, perhaps, the creation of fresh conditions favorable to increased consciousness. Relying on her own reserves, yet acting from a distance, the estranged princess/Shekinah/anima, now alienated from her father, yearns for reintegration into the king/Kether/Self. Yearning, however, is not sufficient. Action must be taken in order to diminish her feelings of alienation.

For harmony to prevail, the king would have to learn to understand the princess's needs and her sensitivity. Thus, he would not only be restoring balance within himself and his kingdom but would, by extension, know fulfillment as father and monarch. The achieving of such a goal necessitates the development of the undervalued feminine aspect of his personality. The shedding of light on his own inadequacies or mood swings could then lead to an increase in his qualitative consciousness.

As a collective soul, the princess/Shekinah/anima is a light-bringing force whose differentiated luminosities will, with the help of the viceroy as ego, slowly infiltrate into the king/Kether/Self complex. It is the viceroy who will journey on an obstacle-ridden course in search of the princess, thereby effectuating the reunification of what has been alienated from the Whole.

The Viceroy as the Questing Ego

When the viceroy/ego realizes the extent of the king's sorrow and introversion, he, as a projection of his sovereign's active and determined side, decides to take matters into his own hands. Having obtained from the king a servant, a horse, and a sum of money, he sets out on his search for the princess.

The hero of Nachman's tale, the viceroy, may be said to represent, according to the Sefiroth, God's ontological principle of Hokhmah (His "wisdom" or *sophia*). Because Kether, the mystery which is the Godhead, is uncognizable, He can be manifested only qualitatively. His actions in the empirical domain are, therefore, both hidden and visible. As Hokhmah, or the "active or determinant principle of knowledge," the viceroy is the first kinetic cause to proceed outward from the Godhead (Schaya 1973, p. 42). He, together with the princess/Shekinah/anima, will ultimately effect a realignment within the Divine archetype.

The viceroy's quest, journey, or pilgrimage, involving arduous forays into vast expanses—deserts, fields, forests—is unfruitful. Yet he persists in his search, deciding to seek a new orientation, not via cogitation but rather through intuition. Setting out on a course without any particular direction, he simply wanders for a period of time until he happens to come upon a beautiful castle surrounded by groups of orderly soldiers. After dismounting from his horse, he is surprised by the fact that instead of being denied access to the magnificent castle by the armed men, he is permitted to enter. Once inside, he wanders from room to room, finally stopping in a hall where a king is seated on a throne. Although soldiers stand guard in an ordered manner, the atmosphere is festive as well as pleasurable: musicians perform and delicacies are served. After tasting the food, the viceroy lies down in a corner of the hall so as to better observe the happenings. The king requests the queen join him, and her throne is placed beside that of the sovereign. Happiness permeates the atmosphere on her entry. The viceroy recognizes her as the lost princess, who is moved by his presence. She explains that she had left her father's kingdom because he had allowed a curse to slip from his mouth. Her return depends on the viceroy's ability to accomplish the following deeds: he must remain in one particular place for a year, during which time he must yearn for her, fast on specific occasions, and on the last day of the time period, must not sleep from sunset to sunset.

Let us now examine the meaning of the tale's symbols. The castle, as enclosure, may be associated with either or both a secure and protective area and a prisonlike fortification. In that the castle which the viceroy enters stands in a remote place, separated from the rest of the world, it gives the impression of being an inaccessible, desirable, and sacred domain. Because Nachman's castle contains both king and queen, a spiritual climate of transcendence may be said to prevail. The king, symbolizing the ruling principle, supreme consciousness, wisdom and self-control, is, at least on the surface, united in harmony with his queen, who represents the most noble feminine values: the capacity for relatedness, understanding, and love. Yet, something seems awry since she mentions to the viceroy her desire to gain her freedom and return to her father's kingdom.

Let us note that the feminine principle was first introduced in Nachman's tale in the person of the princess. When the viceroy sees her in the castle, she is referred to as queen. The change in status since her departure from her father's kingdom suggests some kind of evolution or metamorphosis. As princess, the beautiful and radiant adolescent symbolizes the promise of a supreme or queenly power. Now, as queen, she is identified with Tifereth, representing not only the supernal nature of God's "compassion," but also a mediating power between His complex of attributes. As princess/Shekinah/anima, the lowest in the hierarchy, she had not yet learned to deal with or exercise those latent powers within her being. Indeed, prior to her metamorphosis into the queen, she may well have merited the king's wrath. Was she perhaps stuck in her own childishness, imprisoned in her immaturity? In her capacity as queen, she conveys an impression of completing the existence of the king in the castle, as attested to by the festivities and delicacies and the sense of joy that permeates the atmosphere upon her entrance. Rather than the expression of the childlike and petulant inferior feminine principle, she has now assumed a new dignity. When she and the king sit side by side on their thrones, they do so in seeming equality and balance. Her cognitive side also gives the impression of having evolved. She knows how to find her way: most particularly, when directing the viceroy to take steps to rectify what seems to be wanting in her life.

The Tests

What did the queen/princess have in mind when requesting that the viceroy overcome three different obstacles in order allow her to return with dignity to her father's kingdom, or, mystically and psychologically, to pave the way for her reintegration into the king/Kether/Self dynamic? Would the stress and strain of fulfilling such objectives force a reordering of inner subliminal and rational contents in the king's psyche, thereby breaking the impasse and making whole what had been severed by the princess's departure?

1. Not to travel but to remain in a specific area would indicate a need on the viceroy/Hokhmah/ego's part to experience a period of deep introversion. Meditation and inner probing would help him to come to terms with those turbulent inner components that he, as a projection of the king's ego, allowed to burst forth. An increase in

reflective power would permit the king's ego factor to think before yielding to impulse, the latter having led to the deprecation of what he loved most, his daughter. To ponder, to reason, to deliberate would enable him to strengthen the volatile elements within his being. To acquaint himself with his own potential might help him discover the motivating factors that had given rise to his inner condition of unrest.

2. That the queen/princess/Shekinah/anima asks the viceroy to "yearn" for her in order to free her from bondage in the castle suggests the need for the feeling factor to become increasingly operational. The overly patriarchal king/Kether/Self did not know how to deal with whatever was troubling him with regard to the daughter he so loved. Hurt by his brusqueness and inability to understand her needs, the queen/princess/Shekinah/anima longs for a loving, compassionate, and tender relationship with the ruling principle, qualities the viceroy/Hokhmah/ego, as the king's emissary, must learn to develop within himself. Only then may she be freed from imprisonment within the castle, experienced as a condition of exile from the Godhead.

3. That the viceroy/Hokhmah/ego must not sleep from sunset to sunset suggests that he must learn to be constantly vigilant. If the first two stages of his test are satisfactorily completed, he must no longer look within exclusively but rather focus on the outer world. Extrovertedly, he must remain awake to all possibilities of danger.

Having fulfilled the first two requirements, the viceroy/ Hokhmah/ego, in an optimistic frame of mind, is prepared to meet the third challenge and thereby free the queen/princess/Shekinah/ anima. Just as he is about to accomplish his goal, he sees a tree with luscious apples. His craving for one of them is so strong that he yields to temptation, eats from it, and, predictably, falls into a deep sleep.

The tree may be regarded as an earthly replica of the image of the Sefiroth: Divinity's Ten Emanations are frequently depicted in the form of a tree, associated with the Tree of Life or the Tree of Knowledge. Each of its ten branches symbolizes one of the Divine attributes making up His Totality or Wholeness. The viceroy/ Hokhmah/ego was supposed to fast and not sleep in order to strengthen what had remained undeveloped within him: a sense of vigilance and self-discipline. Because these factors within his personality were wanting, he was unable, at least temporarily, to fulfill this part of his ordeal.

That the viceroy/Hokhmah/ego sleeps rather than remains awake indicates a diminishing, indeed a divestiture, of his powers of differentiation. The new orientation required to free the princess would come to him not from *hypnos*, to use Hesiod's nomenclature, but rather from a twenty-four-hour period of consciousness. Only then would he be able to distinguish good from evil and light from day.

When the viceroy/Hokhmah/ego finally awakens, he asks his servant: "Where am I in the world?" After being told that he has been sleeping for several years, he grieves yet is intent upon making his way to the castle in which the queen/princess/Shekinah/anima lives. He does so. Deeply pained and bitter, she says to him: "If you had only come on that day you would have freed me from here. Because of that one day, you have lost everything. It is true that not eating is very difficult, especially on the last day when the evil impulse waxes strong."

Despite her disappointment, the queen/princess/Shekinah/anima gives the viceroy/Hokhmah/ego another chance to prove himself. He must repeat the first two ordeals. As for the last one, he will now be allowed to eat on the last day but must neither drink nor sleep—"the main thing is [not to] sleep."

The viceroy, determined to complete his tests, accomplishes his goal with regard to the first two. On the last day, however, he sees "a spring gushing forth and it looked red and smelled of wine." He is unable to resist. After tasting the wonderful liquid, he falls into a deep sleep that lasts about seventy years. During this period, but unbeknownst to him, soldiers, carriages, and the queen/princess/Shekinah/anima appear. She stops beside the sleeping viceroy/Hokhmah/ego, but although she shakes him, he fails to awaken. She weeps and bemoans her imprisonment. Removing her kerchief from her head, she writes something on it with her tears, leaves it near the sleeping man, and then rides off.

When the viceroy/Hokhmah/ego finally awakens, his servant tells him what has happened. As he laments, he notices a kerchief and is informed that the queen/princess/Shekinah/anima had left it for him. Raising the kerchief to the sunlight, he allows the letters of the palimpsest to become manifest. Not only does he read of her sorrow, but he is informed of her new whereabouts: she is now living on a golden mountain in a pearly castle.

The kerchief worn around the queen/princess/Shekinah/anima's head symbolizes multiple, mysterious, and unfathomable dimensions.

One of these may allude to the need for greater development of the viceroy's thinking factor. That he had failed to avail himself of a more rational and structured approach to the world, that his determination and will had been wanting, and that he had been prevented from fulfilling his task were directly responsible for the queen/princess/Shekinah/anima's sorrow and tears. Suffering, then, is the medium by which the viceroy/Hokhmah/ego will be moved to act forcefully.

Indeed, it was after imbibing wine—or spirits—that he had succumbed to sleep. Having allowed his cognitive side to become contaminated or deceived by his impulsive and undisciplined physical desires, he had damaged his relationship with the queen/princess/Shekinah/anima. His ordeals had not succeeded in putting him in touch with his innermost essence. Wholeness could not yet be effected. That he failed to live up to his commitment a second time revealed an inability on the ego's part to adhere to the restrictions, prohibitions, and delimitations ordered by the more evolved feminine power.

The Desert Experience

The viceroy again sets out on his quest. This time, however, he leaves his servant behind. That he (the ego) goes alone suggests a need to face those dysfunctional elements within himself, or that part of the Godhead (Self) that needs reorientation. The undertaking of such a lonely journey indicates an increase in the viceroy/Hokhmah/ego's determination to succeed; it also suggests a leap forward in the thinking domain, a need to sort things out for himself. Just as Moses, on a different level, faced God on Mt. Sinai, so the viceroy, as ego, would have to broach the Infinite, as Self.

After traveling in search of the queen/princess/Shekinah/anima, the viceroy/Hokhmah/ego reasoned that the golden mountain and the pearly castle could be found only in an unpopulated area. For him, this meant the desert. The desert experience, which so many holy people throughout the centuries have chosen to undergo, consists of a struggle waged against virtually insurmountable odds and a test of an individual's strength and faith. Because of its isolation, the desert forces a person to face the Self and to grapple with unconscious forces as these are experienced in daily life. The enforced solitude known during the desert experience arouses for some a condition of *metanoia*—the birth of new values, or at least a shift in old ones. The forty years, for example, that the Hebrews spent wandering in the wilderness after their flight from Egypt, the forty days and nights that Jesus spent in the desert after his baptism by John the Baptist, led, in both cases, to a reorientation and renewal.

The Giants

During the viceroy/Hokhmah/ego's search for the queen/princess/ Shekinah/anima, which takes a great deal of time, he finally comes upon a giant or "wild man" carrying a big tree. The giant, who has never seen such a specimen before, asks the viceroy to identify himself: "I am a human being," he replies. He then tells him his story and asks to be directed to the golden mountain. The giant can be of no help in this matter, however, since he has never seen it. "Surely it does not exist at all," he concludes. That the giant tells him it is all an illusion brings tears to the viceroy's eyes. A pleasant sort of fellow, the giant seems to want to help the human being. He tells him that since he is in charge of all animals, and since they roam about the world, at least one may have come across that very special mountain and castle. Thus the animals are summoned and questioned. They answer in the negative: not one has seen such a mountain or castle. "They have deluded you with nonsense," the giant says, urging the viceroy/Hokhmah/ego to turn back. Like Job, however, he will not allow himself to be discouraged and continues on in pursuit of his quest.

In an attempt to help the viceroy/Hokhmah/ego, the giant tells him that his brother, who also lives in the desert, is in charge of all fowls. Flying creatures would surely have seen the mountain and castle from on high. The viceroy/Hokhmah/ego sets out in search of the giant's brother and after many years comes upon another giant who also carries a big tree. Inquiries about the golden mountain and pearly castle are met with the same answer. But, as understanding as his brother, the second giant summons the birds that are under his dominion. Not one has seen such a mountain or castle. The giant advises the viceroy/Hokhmah/ego to visit a third brother who lives deeper in the desert. Since he is in charge of all the winds and since "they roam throughout the whole world," they might know more.

Again the viceroy finds himself wandering for many years in search of the third giant, whom he finally meets. Although he, too, is convinced of the nonexistence of the mountain and the castle, he summons the winds, who again give him a negative answer. The viceroy/Hokhmah/ego is not one to bend: "I know that it surely must exist." At that very moment, another wind arrives and says: "I was detained because I had to transport a princess to a golden mountain and a pearly castle." Overjoyed, the viceroy/Hokhmah/ego is ready to set out once again. The giant, also pleased by the outcome and aware of the long and arduous years ahead for the traveler, gives him a purse filled with money, hoping, he says, to diminish the impact of the burdens he now faces. He then orders the storm wind to carry the viceroy/Hokhmah/ego to the golden mountain upon which stands the pearly castle.

The giant or the gigantic nonhuman entity appearing in many legends and myths (Ymir in the Eddas; Pan Ku in Hsu Cheng's Ancient Chronology; Purusha in the Indian Rigveda) represents the *prima materia* or the world's original substance upon which later generations—or collective souls—build their cultures and civilizations. Because of their immense strength, issuing from the Earth Mother, giants are usually associated with chthonian powers. Their great size and their instinctual natures suggest more brawn than intelligence or spirituality. The presence of the three giants in Nachman's tale, each identified with a different domain—animal, avian, and atmospheric—suggests a hierarchical view of humankind's continuous struggle to fight its natural earthliness in order to evolve spiritually. Nevertheless, according to the *Kabbalah*, humankind cannot count exclusively on celestial forces to experience ascension. Individuals must muster their own powers, tense their own strength in order to triumph over their regressive tendencies.

The three worlds commanded by the giants are in themselves imaged hierarchically: the animal, identified with the telluric sphere; the avian, frequently identified with the soul, with the airy regions; the wind or God's breath and/or spirit, perceived as the ineffable. Only the wind can guide the viceroy/Hokhmah/ego to those vertiginous heights, thereby liberating him from the dross of an inferior instinctual nature. Only in these celestial climes can he rid himself of the imprisoning forces that had led him to succumb to food, water, and sleep.

The viceroy/Hokhmah/ego had to experience all three domains—instinctual, spiritual, and Divine—in order to learn to distinguish or differentiate between the various levels of reality. Although entrapped by his bodily needs prior to the desert experience, his intense faith in his mission sustained him during his difficult trajectory. Faith, without the power to discriminate and then integrate each existing part into the whole, is not sufficiently forceful a catalyst to return the queen/princess/Shekinah/anima to the king/Kether/Self.

Like the tree carried by each of the giants—a symbol of the Sefiroth, or God's Ten Emanations—the viceroy/Hokhmah/ego would also have to learn to reconnect to the Whole. Like the human being, the tree is composed of roots (an instinctual and subliminal sphere); a trunk (a functional or rational world); and branches that rise heavenward (toward the celestial domain where the mystic reaches out to Divinity in a state of *ekstasis*).

To effect a transformation between his potential qualities and a more mature application of his "intelligence" and "wisdom," or Hokhmah, the viceroy had to free the queen/princess/Shekinah/anima. Some mystics, in keeping with such biblical examples as Jacob's ladder (Genesis 28:12), consider the tree as a world axis. An axial image, the tree acts as a connecting agent between earthly and celestial spheres. As metaphor in the psychological domain, it represents the possibility of interaction between the ego, anima, and Self.

The Golden Mountain and the Pearly Castle

Whereas the soldiers of the first castle had allowed the Viceroy/Hokhmah/ego to enter both the city and the edifice, they now refuse him access to the pearly castle. Wiser in the ways of human nature, however, he knows that he must dip his hand into his purse in order to gain entry. He pays his rite of passage, arranging as well for his board once in the new area. He knows a great deal of time must be allotted him to complete this last phase of his test, revealing new and deepened use of his "intelligence and wisdom," or Hokhmah.

Mountain symbolism, like the tree but even more spectacular, is an ascensional image, suggestive of an aerated habitat where wind, as spirit, not only elevates earthly contents but allows one to look out upon the world with greater perspective. Because it is vertical and high in its elevation, the mountain lies closest to heaven and takes on the quality of transcendence. That the mountain in Nachman's tale is golden indicates that we are dealing with the highest of values.

Gold, the purest of metals, is associated with Divinity as well as with the sun. In this regard, it indicates absolute perfection and celestial knowledge. Like the philosopher's stone, it is empowered to transform base into higher or nobler metals. For many mystics as well as psychologists, this treasured "golden body" may purify what is contaminated and transform the unregenerate forces that lie hidden within each human being. That the viceroy/Hokhmah/ego is able to see the golden mountain, which had been invisible to the giants, indicates psychologically that some as-yet unredeemed unconscious contents have finally emerged into the light of consciousness.

In every religion there exists a sacred mountain: Mount Sinai for the Hebrews, the Mount of Olives for the Christians, Mount Meru for the Hindus, Mount Kaf in Islam, K'un-l'un Mountain for the Chinese, Mount Fuji for the Japanese, etc. The combination in Nachman's tale of gold and mountain suggests both a hierophany and a theophany: a meeting place between Divinity and humankind, a union of earth and heaven.

That the castle in which the viceroy/Hokhmah/ego would find the queen/princess/Shekinah/anima was pearly suggests the importance of the water element, associated so frequently with the feminine. It is in water that the pearl, protected by the oyster's shell, gestates. The process of transformation undergone by the pearl, from its inception to its fulfillment, symbolizes creativity. Whereas the gold of the mountain is associated with masculine solar power, the pearl stands for the feminine lunar force. Both may be identified with perfection. It is via the process of a person's search that transmutation may be effected. The viceroy/Hokhmah/ego—having discovered the pearl hidden within its shell and earthly waters during his quest for spiritual beauty, love, and knowledge as inherent in the queen/princess/Shekinah/anima—must now attain higher mountainous regions. For it is in these celestial, cloudy, and vaporous spheres that he will imbibe those spiritual waters, connecting queen/princess/Shekinah/anima with Tifereth, her higher counterpart. A symbol for the sublimation of instincts and the spiritualization of matter, the pearl symbolizes a composite of the most brilliant aspects of the queen/princess/Shekinah/anima in the process of evolution. In that she is consubstantial with the king/Kether/

Self, she as heart, light, and intelligence was the active force driving the viceroy/Hokhmah/ego into fulfilling his mission.

How the viceroy frees the princess, Nachman never reveals to his readers. Nor does he disclose the inward and secret process each person must undergo in order to find his or her center, thereby bringing balance and harmony—at least temporarily—to areas where chaos had once prevailed. As autonomous powers, the queen/princess/Shekinah/anima, along with the viceroy/Hokhmah/ego—both emanations of the central regulating power (king/Kether/Self)—will, for Nachman, govern themselves in accordance with the highest ethical ideals, becoming promoters of peace, justice, and love.

Bibliography

Baynes, H. G. 1969. *Mythology of the Soul*. London: Rider and Company.

Buber, M. 1956. *The Tales of Rabbi Nachman*. Translated by M. Friedman. New York: Horizon Press.

Band, A. J., trans. 1978. *Nahman of Bratslav by Rabbi Ben Simhah Nachman*. New York: Paulist Press.

Schaya, L. 1973. *The Universal Meaning of the Kabbalah*. New York: Penguin.

Scholem, G. 1973. *On the Kabbalah and Its Symbolism*. Translated by R. Manheim. New York: Schocken Books.

———. 1965. *Major Trends in Hebrew Mysticism*. New York: Schocken Books.

Scholem, G., ed. 1963. *Zohar: The Book of Splendor*. New York: Schocken Books.

Agnon's "Edo and Enam"

An Archaeological
Exploration of the
Soul/Psyche

"Edo and Enam" (1950) by S. Y. Agnon,[1] an archaeologist of the soul, narrates the spiritual and psychological drama confronting a young bride, Gemulah, after she has left the land of her ancestors to follow her husband to Jerusalem. A descendent of the ancient tribe of Gad, one of the ten lost tribes of Israel, Gemulah lived with her people in a remote mountain region, perhaps someplace in Southeast Asia. A practitioner of ancient devotional rituals and hymns spoken in a Hebrew long since vanished from the earth, her new environment arouses in her feelings of displacement and alienation. She feels cut off from the world of her origins and the security it had afforded her. More tragically, she mourns the loss of the spiritual and inspirational role she had once played for her people. An irremediable sense of bereavement fills her days. A soul in exile, Gemulah is incapable of adjusting to her new situation and surroundings.

The two male protagonists in "Edo and Enam," Gamzu and Dr. Ginath, are wanderers roaming the earth in search of ancient, "scattered" manuscripts and writings pertaining to their people. The former, a dealer in rare books and texts and a traditionalist in matters of religion, in one of his journeys happened upon a remote mountainous area, where he met and fell in love with a beautiful young girl, Gemulah. A member of the ancient tribe of Gad, she lived the same way as her ancestors who had wanderered there centuries before to escape persecution. Gamzu identifies Gemulah with the moon and stars, that is, with mystical climes. Dr. Ginath, a well-known, open-minded, and scientifically oriented philologist who also travels continuously seeking lost or "scattered" documents relating to his own and other cultures, also fortuitously reaches the area of Gemulah's tribe. Cerebrally inclined, he sets about transcribing the strange grammar and language spoken in this remote region, most importantly, the Enamite hymns that Gemulah sings in the lost Edo language.

Jerusalem: Archetype of the Self

That "Edo and Enam" should be set in the Holy City of Jerusalem suggests a fusion of mystical and empirical worlds. For the pious, Jerusalem is considered the center of God's Creation. It is a sacred zone, a sanctuary of absolute reality, that place where celestial and tellurian forces commune and where light and darkness cohabit. All varieties of life, inanimate and animate, exist inchoate within this microcosm of the macrocosm (Eliade 1974, p. 18). The belief in a heavenly Jerusalem was alluded to by most of the Hebrew prophets (Tobias 13:16; Isaiah 59:1; Ezekiel 60) as well as by the kabbalists. The latter believed that the Holy City was located in the region of the sun, moon, planets, and stars.

Because of their containing, protective, womblike but also limiting qualities, cities in general—and Jerusalem is no exception—have come to symbolize the feminine principle. As a Holy City, however, Jerusalem is identified with Divinity, the masculine principle, and thus may be considered a composite of opposites. Given the right proportions, Jerusalem as a meeting ground of polarities experiences periods of equilibrium; conveyed in psychological terms, of *centeredness* within the personality.

Many Jews living in Jerusalem, then, are said to have rooted themselves within its protective spiritual and empirical boundaries, or hope or intend to do so. Others, living elsewhere and finding themselves alienated from the cultures and ideologies of the lands in which they live, yearn to return to Jerusalem, fully aware of the dangers involved. Still others living in the Diaspora do not consider earthly Jerusalem as home and are content to live in their adopted countries.

As a paradigm for wholeness and centeredness, Jerusalem, for some of the protagonists in "Edo and Enam," may be looked upon psychologically as the central archetype of the Self (total psyche), which encompasses and regulates all the others in the personality. In this capacity, representing an ideal state of wholeness or completion, it makes *holy* or is able to *heal* disparate or exiled contents within the unconscious and conscious realms that might otherwise be torn asunder. As an active ordering center, the archetype of the Self is a suprapersonal authority operating in every individual. It is just this sense of wholeness, completion, and harmony that rootless or wandering Jews ideally yearn for, particularly from the time of their real or symbolic "scattering" or fragmentation in the Diaspora.

Agnon's modern/ancient city of Jerusalem, however, with all of its redemptive and messianic associations, does not represent security and wholeness for all the protagonists in Agnon's tale. Certainly it does for many of the survivors of the Holocaust, as well as for those who have experienced persecution in other lands. Some, however, find themselves psychologically unprepared to find integration within its confines. Not everyone fits the mold, Agnon suggests.

The House: Containment/Imprisonment

The locus of "Edo and Enam" is centered not only in the Holy City of Jerusalem, but in a house. Like the city, the house functions as a centering device and world axis. Set in the valley, separated from the surrounding metropolis, it seems not only to contain a whole world within its walls but is "rimmed with a crown of trees through which beneficent vapors flow, keeping it free from the taint of malign airs" (Agnon 1966, p. 157).

The low-lying valley with its feminine contours may be considered a zone or space receptive to celestial influences. As a cavern like the heart, it not only becomes a receptacle for rhythmical vibrations but is a fertile field for spiritual and psychological events. The valley's circular configuration, "rimmed with a crown of trees," represents the eternal value of spiritual enlightenment. The "crown" ("Kether" for the kabbalist) symbolizes Divinity in His most remote and absolute form.

Like the ancient walled city of Jerusalem, the encircling and protected valley with its house in the center may be looked upon as an aspect of the feminine principle: the repository of occult wisdom and tradition. The house, then, is not only the meeting place of the protagonists, but the matrix, the womb, the locus within which the events are dramatized.

The narrator of the tale, like an impersonal consciousness, visits the owners of the house, Gerhardt and Gerda Greifenbach, who are about to leave for Europe to visit relatives "in the Diaspora." During the course of their conversation, they tell the narrator they are looking for someone to keep an eye on their home. They also tell him that they have rented a room to the world-renowned philologist and ethnologist, Dr. Ginath. Impressed by this scholar's work, the narrator questions them about his "Ninety-nine Words of the Edo language," his "Grammar of Edo," and his transcription and translation of what is considered his great discovery, the Enamite hymns. When the narrator first set eyes on the latter work, he told the Greifenbachs that something deep within him had stirred: "It was the reverberation of a primeval song passed on from the first hour of history through endless generations."

Why was the narrator so impressed by Dr. Ginath's works as a whole and by the Enamite hymns in particular? First, because Dr. Ginath's research had established "a newfound link in a chain that binds the beginnings of recorded history to the ages before." Second, his discovery of the Enamite hymns, with their feminine rhymes and rhythms, disproves previous affirmations that the gods and priests of Enam were male.

The first point discloses the narrator's need to establish a sense of continuity with his ancestors. Such a link is crucial to psychological well-being, particularly for those who have been cut off from their lands and their cultural heritage. In his essay, "The Gifted Child," Jung notes:

Just as the developing embryo recapitulates, in a sense, our phylogenetic history, so the child-psyche relives "the lessons of earlier humanity." The child lives in a prerational and above all in a prescientific world, the world of men who existed before us. Our roots lie in that world and every child grows from those roots. Maturity bears him away from his roots and immaturity binds him to them. Knowledge of the universal origins builds the bridge between the lost and abandoned world of the past and the still largely inconceivable world of the future. How should we lay hold of the future, how should we assimilate it, unless we are in possession of the human experience which the past has bequeathed to us? Dispossessed of this, we are without root and without perspective, defenseless dupes of whatever novelties the future may bring. (Quoted in von Franz 1972, p. 203)

Historical continuity, as Jung suggests, connects an individual to the archetypal foundations of his or her psyche. Rooting in this manner acts as a safeguard: it prevents a person from being carried away by illusions and delusions or from a disintegration of the personality. To be divested of emotional support is to invite an atomization or dissociation of the psyche, as in schizophrenia. Under such circumstances, increasing fragmentation may lead to an eclipse of the ego, overwhelmed as it could be by the power of autonomous unconscious complexes.

So important is the motif of continuity to the stability of the psyche that in most religious texts (from Hesiod's *Theogony*, to the *Mahabharata*, to the Maya Quiche's *Popul Vuh*, to the Bible) genealogies of gods, kings, and ancestors establish a link with the beginnings of nations and their godheads. Such connections with a past make concrete what has seemingly vanished into oblivion, thus giving order, orientation, and a sense of unity where otherwise chaos would prevail.

The names of Agnon's protagonists all begin with the letter G, the first letter of the Hebrew word *galut* ("exile," "Diaspora") emphasizing the harrowing need of these wandering beings to root themselves, to find some kind of bond with a mythical past, *in illo tempore*, thus endowing themselves with feelings of security and belonging. Not one of the participants in Agnon's tale is settled, not one is whole, not one lives in harmony with himself or herself.[2]

Wandering Scholars

What kind of man is the internationally famous scholar Dr. Ginath? Secretive, in that he deals with ancient, esoteric, frequently undeciphered documents. A wanderer, in his continuous search for written texts or oral material that might reveal information concerning ancient tongues and primordial civilizations. A thinking type, because of the objective and scientific manner in which he goes about acquiring and recording information. Perception and judgment are most important to him in his continuous quest to define objects and things with regard to name and concept. Rational, he proceeds in the most detached and determined of ways in reaching his goal. Never, however, does he allow himself to become emotionally involved. Never remaining for more than a night or two in one place, he leads a virtually nomadic existence that precludes any kind of bonding. Is it an excuse to escape commitment?

A restless man, Dr. Ginath is forever driven by his intellect. His world, revolving solely around the mind, has divested itself of the feeling function. So repressed or unused is the feeling side of his personality that it has virtually atrophied. Dr. Ginath not only has cut himself off from any and all human relationships but is even unaware of the existence of others. Eros is missing from his world.

Dr. Ginath, a delver into esoteric matters, is himself a man of mystery. When, for example, the inquisitive narrator learns that the Greifenbachs had heard a woman's voice, singing and speaking in a strange tongue and emanating from Dr. Ginath's room, he is intrigued. Because any entertaining of others was specifically forbidden and the woman communicated in an incomprehensible language, he wondered whether Dr. Ginath had created her. Such things are said to have occurred, as in the case of the golem.

Greifenbach then told the narrator that Dr. Ginath had given him and his wife a gift of extraordinary value: two parched brown leaves with strange lines and markings on them, which he kept in an iron box. Were they written in some secret code, he wonders? Although they look like nothing more than tobacco leaves, Dr. Ginath had specifically told them at the time that they were talismans from a distant land and had said no more about them.

After the Greifenbachs depart for Europe, the narrator keeps his promise and decides to spend a night or two in their house. One evening, he is awakened from his sleep by a strange scratching at the door. He opens it and recognizes his old friend, Gabriel Gamzu. A scholar like Dr. Ginath, Gamzu also spends his time traveling to distant, inaccessible lands in search of ancient texts. Strange things have happened to him. Since his marriage to Gemulah, Gamzu's life has changed drastically. He has given up traveling, devoting his every waking hour to nursing his bedridden wife. Rather than being grateful to her husband for his kindness, she, perhaps compelled by some inner rage, tears his clothes and scratches his face.

How and why did Gamzu come to the Greifenbach's house when he did not even know them? Nor had he had any idea that the narrator was spending the night there; it had been a spur-of-the-moment decision. After returning from the synagogue, Gamzu tells his friend, he discovered that his paralyzed wife was no longer at home. How is such a phenomenon possible? the narrator asks. "Every night when the moon is full, my wife gets up from bed and walks to wherever the moon leads her," Gamzu answers. Even though he locks the doors and windows, Gemulah finds a way of escaping.

Somnambulism, a complex operation of the psyche, has haunted the imaginations of scientists and writers since early times. Shakespeare's Lady Macbeth reenacted fragments of her crime while sleepwalking at night; Kleist gave his readers a literary description of somnambulism in his play *Das Käthchen von Heilbronn* (1810). In the eighteenth century, the Marquis de Puységur, Mesmer's student, concluded after experimentation that a universal fluid (electricity) could permeate a human body and endow it with extraordinary powers, even clairvoyance. Scientists have classified some types of somnambulism among hysterical illnesses.

Gemulah may have been a hysteric, stimulating unconsciously an organic disease leading to her paralysis, sleepwalking, and aphasia. A victim of overdominant subliminal contents, she has allowed her consciousness to be virtually deprived of its ability to function. Dissociation of mental or bodily functions such as Gemulah experiences invite fragmented energy packets to operate autonomously in the psyche. The weakened ego complex, no longer in a position to channel disruptive elements, is unable to integrate explosive or disruptive facets of the psyche and thus permits the hyperactivity of dissociative phenomena such as split-offs and hysteria to dominate.

The somnambulist—suffering, as we shall see, from a dissociative disorder—is possessed of a double personality. Somnambulistic fugues or wanderings may be precipitated, scientists claim, by the freeing of blocked or repressed emotions, forbidden wishes, impulses, or prohibitions, and the memory of traumatic events the psyche is unable to face. Gemulah's psychogenic reaction to what she experiences as an intolerable situation compels her to seek gratification in some mysterious manner.

The question now remains as to how and why Gamzu went to the Greifenbachs' house. His response is: "Going to the south, turning to the north, turning goes the wind, and again to its circuits the wind returns." Was he, too, showing symptoms of hysteria? Was he perhaps enslaved by an *idée fixe*? By an obsessive or autochthonous idea? A thinking disorder interfering with his psychological functioning?

So traumatized had Gamzu felt upon finding his wife's bed empty that he was suddenly deprived of any sense of recall. Living as he did on such an archaic level of the psyche, he had incorporated the object of his thought (his wife) into his ego (center of consciousness), which he then projected onto the outside world. Because his normal state of consciousness had been suppressed, he has no voluntary ego awareness or any memory of his action.

A deeply religious man, Gamzu tells the narrator that he had been led to the Greifenbachs' home by some extraterrestrial force. The word *wind*, as he uses it, evokes biblical imagery: wind (*ruach*) is synonymous with the Spirit of God (*breath*), as it had moved over the primordial waters prior to the Creation (Genesis 1:2) and as "it breathed a living soul into Adam" (Genesis 2:7). Wind is also said to have lifted up Elijah, bringing him to the heavenly realm (2 Kings 2:11) (Kaplan 1988, pp. 42, 49). Psychologically, when wind is strong or agitated, it reveals an unconscious condition of turmoil and instability as well as a yearning to supplant inner chaos with the comfort of cosmos.

Gamzu, along with his wife, is indeed psychologically troubled. His name reveals the personality he would like to possess. An ancient Aramaic word meaning "to graft" in fig culture, *gamzu*, describes an individual who intends to bring together (or graft) disparate factors of spirit and psyche with the understanding of integrating these into the whole. The unresolved dichotomies (feminine and masculine, rational and irrational, past and present, Orthodox and Reformed) within Gamzu's psyche have been pulling him apart (Hochman 1970, p. 66).

So involved had Gamzu become in his continuous travels and searchings for ancient volumes and first editions that the inner schism created by his divided and uncentered pulsations had not yet surfaced. Libido had been and still was repressed, exploding only in times of duress and then manifesting itself solely in affective charges. Limited to a patriarchal environment with intellect or logos prevailing, he, like Dr. Ginath, had no time for eros. As a result, his experience with women was virtually nil, nor did he feel the need of developing such relationships. Vulnerable to the extreme, Gamzu had been unable to handle the emotions that had erupted upon his first seeing Gemulah in her mountain environment. No confrontation with the volatile passion she aroused in him occurred, no integration of these emotions into the personality as a whole took place. Overwhelmed by her presence, he became her servant and votary.

The funneling of Gamzu's libido from one extreme (rejection of eros) to its opposite (obsession with eros) had eliminated the energetic tension inherent in a healthy personality. Thus did he become the victim of *enantiodromia*: "when one pair of opposites becomes excessively predominant in the personality, it is likely to turn into its opposite" (Edinger, p. 2). Unlike Dr. Ginath, a cerebral, steady, logical, and detached fellow, Gamzu was fundamentally emotional. His behavior was affective, erratic, and, as suggested earlier, even showed symptoms of hysteria.

Gemulah: Moon, Virgo, Angel

Gamzu first saw Gemulah after following complicated sea routes then walking forty days in a desert wilderness where he was caught in a sandstorm that blinded him in one eye, whereupon he was finally picked up by a caravan that brought him to a remote area high in the mountains, to the ancient tribal community of Gad ("good fortune" in Hebrew).

That Gamzu spent forty days in the wilderness, as Moses had upon the summit of Mt. Sinai, is significant; forty is a number used countless times in both the Old and New Testaments. The forty days has been prolonged to forty years in the biblical texts, as in the desert wanderings of the Israelites prior to their arrival in the Holy Land (Numbers 32:13). The ordeals experienced are to be understood mythically, as part of an initiation process leading an erstwhile hero to spiritual and psychological development. Would Gamzu's trials expand his consciousness? Would he learn to relate to Gemulah rather than merely idolize her?

When Gevariah, Gemulah's father, realized how ill Gamzu was upon his arrival, he prepared charms that would heal him. Although Gamzu recovered, his eye had been destroyed during the desert sandstorm. He would remain blind and thus deprived, from a symbolic point of view, of his intuitive and perceptive faculties. His ability, therefore, to confront overwhelming emotional factors would diminish, as would his ability to evaluate, differentiate, or objectify situations and people.

When he first met Gevariah and Gemulah, the two captivated his every thought. His fascination was most potent during the twilight hours, when listening to them converse in both ancient Hebrew and in a secret language of their own creation. In the evening, when the sun's power (compared so frequently with the rational sphere) declines, the earth becomes enclosed in dimmer lunar luminosities (associated with subliminal spheres). It was then that Gamzu's fantasies roamed with increasing vigor. The sight of Gemulah seated with a white kid in her lap and of her father standing nearby, an eagle hovering over his head, transported Gamzu into a state of virtual ecstasy.

Because the goat is associated with lunar spheres (Numbers 28:22), and the eagle with God (Exodus 19:4), the two were identified in Gamzu's mind not with individuals per se but with collective powers. It was as if father and daughter belonged to a mythical past: they were capable of connecting him with his ancestors, thus instilling in him the feelings of well-being that he so desperately needed.

Although mesmerized by Gemulah's outer beauty and gracious bearing, it was her voice, with all of its ancient rhythms, cadences, and feeling tones, that affected him most deeply. The music emanating from her mouth was like a sounding board for conflating celestial and terrestrial fluidic forces, for exciting electric currents, with all their affective charges, to act on his nerves and psyche. "And when she sang, her voice stirred the heart like that of the bird Grofith, whose song is sweeter than that of any creature on earth."

Gemulah's strange song was also semantically alluring to Gamzu; its hidden meanings drew him ever more powerfully to her as an occult force. Her diapasons and phrases served to hypnotize and intoxicate him, thus increasing her hold over his world and cutting him off still more powerfully from the everyday domain. Unlike the sirens of old (as depicted by Homer, Aristotle, Pliny, Ovid, Heine, etc.), Gemulah had no intention of catching the unsuspecting Gamzu in her web. Rather, it was Gamzu who succumbed to the numinousness of his vision and the subtle rhythms and tones of her song, when gazing at her "poised on a rock at the top of a mountain which not every man could climb, with the moon lighting up her face while she sang, *Yiddal, yiddal, yiddal, vah, pah, mah.*" Likewise, according to the kabbalists, did the Shekinah in exile sing songs and hymns to her beloved husband, God (Scholem 1973, p. 148).

Amazed and transfixed, Gamzu likened Gemulah to one of the angels of the Divine Presence who unites with the Divine Being. The image before him worked like a narcotic on his conscious judgment, nullifying it to the point where instinct alone dominated.

Gamzu was *blind* to the fact that Gemulah was a collective figure and immune to any personal relationship. As indicated by her name, which means "the reciprocal or the reciprocated one," she cannot give of herself, nor can she fulfill Gamzu's unrealistic expectations of her. His lack of psychological development, his utter inexperience with nonpersonal eros, makes him especially susceptible to the power she exudes when standing on the mountain peak bathed in the luminosity of moon rays (Harding 1971, p. 119). So taken was Gamzu by Gemulah that he immediately went to her father to ask for her hand in marriage.

Why should Gamzu have acted so precipitously? Several factors may serve to explain his affective reactions. He connected the feminine figure he saw etched against the heavens with paradise and the primordial experience of oneness. The intensity of his feeling of belonging and of being enveloped in the Divine Sphere, when heretofore he had felt at loose ends, uprooted, and homeless, enabled him to experience the sense of blissful unity a child knows: that *participation mystique* that is the avowed enemy of any developing ego. His archaic vision of Gemulah—bewitching, alluring, and instilling him with a sense of great joy and comfort—is also death-dealing. If one is caught up in its seductive and devouring aspect, regression and stagnation could readily ensue (Neumann 1986, p. 11).

To be submerged by admiration, to be bewitched by a spell or an illusion, debilitates the power of reason and of evaluation. No confrontation with the feminine principle, which could be instrumental in detaching Gamzu from his vision's impress, is forthcoming, nor can any development of his own individuality be expected. As long as he remains mesmerized by what he perceives to be the most sublime of beings, his incipient ego remains vulnerable to destruction. Important as well is that his ungoverned unconscious and his uncontrollable emotionality allow archetypal imagery—the dominance of a moon figure—to flood his psyche (ibid., p. 11). Mountain symbolism, on the other hand, reveals the presence of a counterforce in the personality; Gamzu's need for the patriarchal realm and for ego development. Heights, by their very verticality, convey transcendence, spirituality, sacredness; a mountain's mass expresses a power principle. In many religious traditions, mountains have been identified with theophanies and hierophanies: Olympus, Meru, Tabor, Olives, Kaf, Fuji, etc. The mountain peak on which Gevariah stands may be viewed as the closest point of contact between heaven and earth and as an example of a human being's ascensional needs. Gamzu's sense of urgency, albeit unconscious, indicates a need for finding some figure associated with the heavenly sphere who would not only accept and care for his wandering soul but endow it with wisdom. Unwilling to bind or limit himself to earthly matters alone, Gamzu, like Dr. Ginath, had rejected a life of enslavement to a world of commitment. Their search kept taking them elsewhere.

Gemulah and her father seemingly fulfilled all of Gamzu's needs. They belonged to their landscape and they experienced their attachment to their distant mountains as David had: as a stronghold of security and comfort in time of trouble. "Lord, by thy favor thou has made my mountain to stand strong: thou didst hide thy face, and I was troubled. . . . Thou has turned for me my mourning into dancing . . . and girded me with gladness; . . . To the end that my glory may sing praise of thee" (Psalm 30:7, 11, 12).

Unlike most women identified with the moon, Gemulah does not live in a grove, spring, or grotto, areas where water trickles down. Nor, as is the case with many of her predecessors, is she associated with moisture or fertility. Her habitat is the mountain. Her constellation is the moon, referring not to the body but to the spirit. Let us recall in this connection that Mount Sinai, where God gave Moses the Tablets of the Law, is translated as Mountain of the Moon (Harding 1971, p. 54).

In ancient Hebrew tradition, the changing aspect of the moon was equated with a nomadic and continuously modified itinerant existence. Its association in Agnon's tale, then, with members of the tribe of Gad and other biblical figures, is analogous. Adam, let us recall, was the first to begin a life of wandering (Genesis 3:24); Cain, the builder of the first city, was destined to the life of a vagabond after his crime (Genesis 4:14); Abraham received God's commandment to leave his father's land and home (Genesis 13:1). The lives of these and other religious exiles, prefigurations of the Diaspora, may be likened to Gamzu's peripatetic existence (Scholem 1973, p. 105).

That Gamzu identifies the feminine principle with the moon is also in keeping with the religious beliefs of multiple nations from time immemorial (witness the moon goddesses Hathor, Isis, Artemis, Astarte, Mary, etc.). To associate a constellation with a human being, however, is to endow that person with spiritual and nonearthly qualities and with collective and nonindividual attributes. As already suggested, Gemulah, as experienced by Gamzu, has no identity, no ego, and is not flesh and blood. She lives in Gamzu's psyche as an aspect of matriarchal consciousness. In that the moon passively reflects the sun's rays, it stands for the indirect, unmanifested, and occult side of knowledge as well as for the cold, impassive feminine nature. Gemulah is just that. Her connection with the moon transforms her into a measurer, not of abstract quantitative but of qualitative time, with its periods and rhythms, its waxings and wanings. The mysterious connection between the lunar cycle and the woman's biological rhythms (the twenty-eight-day cycle), which conditions to a great extent physical and psychological life, has both positive and negative, or light and chthonian, aspects. Equated with the unconscious, the moon, like the dream, represents that pale, barely illuminated side of life that emerges at night.

As mentioned in the chapter on Rabbi Nachman, the "ambivalent" or dark side of the moon, when associated with the Shekinah, is also identified with the notion of exile. Whereas in the Talmud, God is present wherever the Hebrews are driven, in the *Kabbalah*, when persecution forces them to wander, *a part of God Himself is exiled from God*. Such an exile within the Godhead, as represented in mystical texts, is virtually personified: it is tantamount to the banishment of the queen or the daughter of the king by her husband or father. The abyss between the feminine and masculine principles within the Godhead, then, indicates a projection of the duality existing within the hearts and minds of those forced out of their lands. The Shekinah's exile, during the waning moon, further indicates a degradation of status, a robbing of her light to the point of becoming the "lightless receiver of light" (Scholem 1973, pp. 107, 108). For this reason, prior to the birth of the new moon, prayers or repentance and fasting were called for by the pious; after its rebirth, prayers of joy. When God was once again reunited with his Shekinah, the inner division gave way to a condition of original unity and harmony, which then flowed unimpeded throughout the cosmos (Isaiah 30:26).

On a psychological plane, God's separation or exile from his Shekinah, or his feminine principle, suggests a deprivation or rejection of his anima (an autonomous psychic content or inner woman in man). To reject an anima or soul force is to divest oneself of one's guide or inspiration. Living in a strictly patriarchal sphere, both Gamzu and Dr. Ginath had obliterated any workable eros force, any capacity to relate, to feel deeply for another human being. When Gamzu sees Gemulah on top of the rock, with moonbeams shining all about, he experiences her as a function: a sublime, idealized, untouchable abstraction. As anima, she takes on the allure of a mysterious, autonomous force projected onto spatial heights. Looking up to her, he is drawn away from his earthbound connection and distracted from his own focus in life. His idolization of Gemulah encourages him to lead an increasingly passive and withdrawn existence, thus trampling and crushing whatever remains of his individuality and creative élan.

That Gamzu equates Gemulah with an angel, an evanescent creature fluttering about in the air, is yet another indication of his atomization of his anima. He has an unconscious fear of being trapped by an earthly woman and desires to flee all commitment such a relationship demands. Angels, traveling from the heights to the depths of astral spheres, are messengers, as the Greek word *angelos* suggests. Their functions are multiple: they are destroyers (2 Samuel 24:16), interpreters of God's messages (Job 3:23), and protectors (Genesis 19). Gemulah is, for Gamzu, a mediating force between celestial and earthly spheres, an invisible transformative principle.

That Gamzu equates Gemulah with Virgo, one of the twelve signs of the zodiac, suggests a transformation of primordial energy from unity or the nonformal (within God or an individual) to multiplicity or the formal (as a constellation in the heavens). Virgo's visibility, then, indicates her fall into matter or existence, her exile from the Godhead, and her yearning to return to the world of the absolute.

As Virgo ("virgin"), anima, or soul image, Gemulah must remain unblemished, ethereal, and sublimated. She can, therefore, thrive only as a projection, never as an earthly woman. Like the Shekinah when exiled from God, Virgo, if banished from her habitat, will either die or become a negative power, or both.

The Archetypal Spiritual Father

Gevariah, Gemulah's father, could have been a positive archetypal father figure for Gamzu. But Gamzu had been unable to objectify his reaction to this sublime, formidable, and awesome figure. Instead, he was transfixed by Gevariah, a spiritual force, particularly when standing, as had Gemulah, on the highest of mountainous peaks: "A sky-blue turban on his head, his complexion and beard set off by his flowing hair, his dark eyes shining like two suns, his feet bare and the color of gold." Gevariah had, Gamzu said, the face of a lion, the strength of a bull, and the lightfootedness of an eagle in flight. The three biblical epithets with which Gevariah is endowed reveal the incredible energy constellated by this figure in Gamzu's psyche: the lion, a sovereign solar symbol, known as the king of animals, is identified with Judah (Genesis 49:9); the bull with strength and power (Jeremiah 50:11); the eagle with the masculine, spiritual, and fiery nature of the sun image (Job 9:26, 39:27).

Gevariah[3] has multiple virtues: he leads his people in prayer, he heals the sick, writes charms, teaches the young girls the dances and songs of their people, and forges the weapons for the tribe. Gemulah is Gevariah's mainstay. After his wife died in childbirth, he took no other, preferring to pass his esoteric knowledge down to his daughter. The father-daughter identification experienced by Gamzu was so powerful that his weakly structured ego was overwhelmed by its energetic charge. Frozen, as if caught in a spell, Gamzu was incapable of coping with anything remotely connected to the empirical domain. His inner world was transformed into a blank space, immobilizing whatever healthy instinctual reactions might have helped him. Had Gamzu undergone a numinous experience, an epiphany, unconsciously envisioning the father-daughter complex as God and His Shekinah?

The day Gamzu asked for Gemulah's hand in marriage, Gevariah took him to the highest of the steepest mountains, then dug beneath a certain rock, lifted the stone that blocked access to a cave, went inside and removed a bundle of dry leaves from an earthenware jar, saying,

> There is magic in them . . . as long as they remain in your hands you may control Gemulah's steps so that she will not go astray. . . . So, when the nights of the full moon come, take these plants and set them in the window facing the door, and hide them so that no man will notice them, and I assure you that if Gemulah leaves the house she will return to you before the moon returns to her proper sphere.

Strange characters had been written on these leaves, Gamzu noted. As for their colorations, they were unrecognizable: mixtures of gold, azure, purple, and the primary colors of the rainbow, all of which altered with silvery moon strands and tones of seaweed as if drawn from the depths of the sea.

Before Gamzu's marriage took place, he went to Vienna to see if his blind eye could be made to see. It could not. Upon his return to

Gemulah's mountain region, he sensed that something had changed. What it was, he did not know. He had been told, nevertheless, that a holy man, a Hacham Gideon of Jerusalem, had stayed with Gevariah's tribe for six months, that he had healed the sick, alleviated much suffering, and had recorded Gemulah's songs and conversations in his notebook. Then, one day, as Gevariah walked to the mountain top in an attempt to learn from the eagles how they renew their youth, one of the birds of prey attacked and mauled him with his talons. Neglecting his wounds, Gevariah grew steadily worse, remaining alive only to witness and direct the seven nights of dancing, singing, and feasting celebrating his daughter's wedding.

Gemulah's Diaspora

Only after a year of mourning did Gemulah agree to leave her land and make the long, hard journey by caravan and ship to Israel. Gamzu's return to Jerusalem indicated a step toward wholeness; for Gemulah, it meant living in Diaspora. Excision from her native soil could only lead to catastrophe. Her ancestral home, symbolizing for her sustenance and support, had suddenly vanished. As if standing on thin air now, Gemulah's rock of generations, which had endowed her with the solidity and energy needed to pursue her work as her father's daughter and as inspiration for her tribe, had suddenly been withdrawn. Undone, divested of her original roots and function, she no longer felt a sense of continuity. Her ancestral soul had been banished, the spiritual power she had inherited from her father and his father before him, giving her life dignity and purpose, had been drained. Dissociated from the archetypal foundations of her psyche, she no longer had a collective role to play for her people, nor was she the bearer of her father's secret wisdom. What remained? To be an incompetent wife.

Because of the father-daughter identification, Gemulah related, psychologically, to paternal logos: the spiritual male force within her (animus), characterized by cognition. As a female replica of paternal spiritual knowledge, she had been endowed, as had her father, with intense energetic tension, that is, with numinousness. Because she had been her father's helpmate, she had been looked upon as a kind of high priestess for the tribe of Gad, a community of lost souls.

Once she had relocated in Jerusalem, Gemulah was incapable of facing her now-empty existence. A vast and fearful void opened up before her. Divested of her spiritual mission and with no love or sexual longing for her husband, nothing could fill the seemingly infinite vacuum that cannibalized her being. Depression and illness set in; song and speech were withheld. Inwardness and motor aphasia led to depression. The withdrawal of libido from the empirical world and its introjection into the unconscious led to a concomitant loss of interest in any and all activities in the empirical domain. Blackness prevailed in her silent, cold, remote, and unfathomable inner realm.

Always her father's daughter, Gemulah had never been able to develop into an independent woman. Tied as she was to the patriarchal sphere, she had always adjusted her individuality to the will and needs of the collective. Regression is implicit in such a relationship, based as it is on an unconscious self-renunciation and perhaps even a suicidal tendency. That Gemulah passively accepted such a role in life indicated her ego's fascination with her father's mythical world.

Just as struggle and confrontation were lacking when Gamzu projected the form of Gemulah onto his anima, so the same may be said to have happened to Gemulah, dominated as she was by her animus, represented by her father. As such, she was contained in the collective world of the tribe and therefore was and would always be her father's daughter.

Both Gamzu and Gemulah reacted to their unconscious condition of psychological stasis instinctually and affectively. Gemulah, however, was continuously driven back to the spiritual domain of the father archetype—adding inertia to an already passive and poorly structured ego and a fear of and inability to relate to the outside world. No transition to independence could come to pass nor could there be any progressive development of the ego without struggle or fight. Because she never developed her own feminine side, she existed as an extension of her father: logos, spirit, sublimation, etherealness.

When Gamzu, married and living in Jerusalem at the time, discovers that the leaves Gevariah had given him have been lost and that Gemulah, on the night of the full moon, has not returned home, he tells the narrator that not long ago he had sold some ancient texts and he thinks the precious leaves may have been mixed in with them. Just as they had disappeared, so had his power over Gemulah's somnambulism vanished.

As Gamzu informs the narrator that his wife is nowhere to be found, his facial features alter: they resemble "formless clay," as if he had suddenly been divested of his soul. As if unconsciously propelled to do so, he turns his head toward the door, the window, and the wall. Voices are heard. A strange language is being spoken. Gamzu rushes to Dr. Ginath's anteroom. The narrator follows. Both are greeted by an incredible sight: moonlight fills the room as Gemulah, wrapped in white, in a somnambulant trance, speaks to her spiritual lover—Dr. Ginath—in her esoteric tongue. He is seated at a table and takes down her every word.

Reminiscent in some ways of Wagner's motif in *The Flying Dutchman* and of Ibsen's *Lady from the Sea*, in which heroines await the arrival of the "stranger" to experience their great love, so Gemulah serves her beloved as she once had her father: as logos. Had she lived out her passion concretely, she might have detached herself from her father's image or transferred its archetypal power to that of her lover. In a somnambulant trance, however, she was not conscious of what she was doing or speaking. In love with Dr. Ginath, the Hacham Gideon who had visited her land when Gamzu was away in Vienna, the vulnerable and inexperienced Virgo side of her character prevailed. Like Gamzu, she is acted upon, not actor. Panic-stricken by what he sees, and fearful of losing his soul or what he considers to be his love, Gamzu rushes toward Gemulah and flings his arms around her waist. She draws back, calling to Hacham Gideon—Dr. Ginath, in reality—who tells her she must follow her husband. She begs to be allowed to remain with Dr. Ginath, maintaining that she is no one's wife and promising to sing the song of the Grofith bird, which can only be sung once in a lifetime, after which it dies. He still refuses. Gamzu grabs her weakened body and takes her home.

There she remains, but only until the moon has completed its cycle. Once it shines anew and in all of its radiance, she, like the Shekinah, seeks to unite with her beloved. From an article that the narrator happens to read in a newspaper, the reader learns that tragedy has ensued. An eyewitness account reports the death of Dr. Ginath, who had gone out of his room to rescue a woman climbing to the roof. When he rushed up to her, however, the parapet collapsed and both fell to their deaths.

Neither Dr. Ginath nor Gemulah could have met a different fate in Agnon's parable. She existed for her scholar lover as she had for her father and for Gamzu: as logos. In Diaspora, she had been divested of her function as inspiration to her people; thus she was cut off from her purpose and goal in life. Attempting to resume her role as logos for her scholar lover and failing to do so, she felt bereaved. Spirit had been cut off from its lifeline. Gemulah, who had never existed as a flesh-and-blood human being but only as a disembodied voice going back to the beginning of time, never died because she never lived. Redeemed, she had returned from her exile and united with her beloved in the written word. Gemulah is voice; Dr. Ginath, transcriber. The books resulting from their oneness have been disseminated throughout the world: "Anyone who is not blind, anyone who has the power to see, readily makes use of his light."

Notes

1. Samuel Joseph Agnon (1888–1970) was the first Hebrew writer to receive the Nobel Prize for Literature (1966). Born in Buczacs, Galicia, he was brought up in a deeply religious family. After emigrating to Palestine in 1907, the family changed its name to Agnon. Following a year spent in Europe, Agnon returned in 1913 to Jerusalem, which he made his permanent home. His tales and novels, such as *Bridal Canopy* and *And the Crooked Shall Become Straight* are known for their simple yet profound meanings, their insights into character, their ironies and subtle humor as well as their pathos.

2. Agnon's pseudonym was derived from the Hebrew word *aginut* (bereavement). The title of his first story was "Agunot" (1908), suggesting solitude and a universal failure to find fulfillment.

3. *Gevaria* has two parts in Hebrew: *gever* meaning man, strength, power; the suffix *iah* is the name of God. *Gevariah*, then, might be translated as the "strength of God." Told to me by Dr. Paul Neumarkt, scholar, poet, and editor of *Evolutionary Psychology*.

Bibliography

Agnon, S. Y. 1966. *Two Tales by S. Y. Agnon*. Translated by Walter Lever. New York: Schocken Books.

Edinger, E. "Outline of Analytical Psychology." Unpublished paper.

Eliade, M. 1974. *The Myth of the Eternal Return*. Princeton, N.J.: Princeton University Press.

Harding, E. 1971. *Woman's Mysteries*. New York: G. B. Putnam & Sons.

Hochman, B. 1970. *The Fiction of S. Y. Agnon*. Ithaca, N.Y.: Cornell University Press.

Jung, C. G. 1950. *Symbols of Transformation. CW*, vol. 5. Translated by R. F. C. Hull. New York: Pantheon Books.

———. 1957. *Psychiatric Studies. CW*, vol. 1. Translated by R. F. C. Hull. Princeton, N.J.: Princeton University Press, 1970.

Kaplan, A. 1988. *Meditation and Kabbalah*. York Beach, Maine: Samuel Weiser Books.

Neumann, E. 1956. The moon and matriarchal consciousness. In *Dynamic Aspects of the Psyche: Selections from Past Springs*. New York: The Analytical Psychology Club of New York, 1964.

———. 1986. Fear of the feminine. *Quadrant* 19,1:7–30.

Scholem, G. 1973. *On the Kabbalah and Its Symbolism*. New York: Schocken Books.

von Franz, M.-L. 1972. *Creation Myths*. Zurich: Spring Publications.

I. B. Singer's "Yentl the Yeshivah Boy"

The Talmud and Gender Deconstruction

"Yentl," a short story by Isaac Bashevis Singer (1904–1991), dramatizes the events confronting a young girl from an orthodox Polish family as she attempts to break out of an ultrapatriarchal society. The struggle waged by the protagonist, Yentl, which takes place toward the end of the nineteenth or in the early twentieth century, is all the more acute because of her need to remain *true* to her nature. She brings sorrow upon herself and those she loves in her desire to circumvent rigid spiritual and social conditions, but the crux of the tale lies in her determination and perseverance in pursuing her quest.

Because of Yentl's resolve and steadfastness, she may be likened to the ancient judge, Deborah. Unlike other biblical woman, Deborah was not known primarily for her relationship to a man, as was the case of Abraham's wife Sarah, or Moses' sister Miriam. Deborah's fame rested on her own merits. Although Yentl might never make a name for herself, she nevertheless remains the prototype of the woman seeking to divest herself of intellectual constriction. That she was endowed with an indomitable will and accepted psychological pain in standing her ground brings to mind Job's assertion to God: "Though He slay me, yet will I trust in Him: but I will maintain my own ways before Him" (Job 13:15). As God had allowed Satan to test Job's righteousness by visiting upon him excruciating suffering, the satanic elements erupting in Yentl's psyche, although inflicting emotional distress, have a positive effect on her, catalyzing her to complete her rite of passage.

Following the deaths of first her mother, then her father, Yentl made the momentous decision to move away from Yanev, her native town. It was not that she felt lonely or had not been solicited by marriage brokers; relatives and friends had urged her to accept a husband and begin a family. She had other plans. Very much her father's daughter, Yentl was keenly aware of her likes and dislikes. She had always found distasteful the performing of women's chores: cooking, knitting, sewing, and "chatting with silly women." Moreover, she functioned poorly in the home, burning and spoiling whatever dishes she made. Underneath it all, she rejected the entire social structure of the community. Not only were women relegated to the home, they were imprisoned and barred from acquiring higher religious learning.

As long as Yentl's father, Reb Todros, had been alive, life seemed to her idyllic. Daily, after seeing to it that the door of the house was locked and the windows curtained, father and daughter spent hours studying the Torah. So excellent a pupil was she that her father said to her: "Yentl—you have the soul of a man."

"So why was I born a woman?" she responds.

"Even Heaven makes mistakes," he says.

That Yentl's father had told her she had the "soul of a man," thereby equating the thinking function with the masculine gender, was an appropriate view in his time.

Yentl understood at an early age that it would be inimicable to her nature to follow in her mother's or any woman's footsteps. Men's activities alone suited her. First and foremost, she was passionately interested in learning. In time, she realized that she was physically different from others of her sex—tall, thin, "with small breasts and narrow hips." Nor could the games she played as a child be categorized as women's amusements. When, for example, her father took his afternoon nap, she used to put on his clothes, including his skull cap and velvet hat, then looked at herself in the mirror. With great satisfaction, she found that "she looked like a dark, handsome young man." In fact, "there was even a slight down on her upper lip." Her braids alone revealed her gender. And these could be easily cut. "Secretly, she had even smoked her father's long pipe."

When Yentl's father used to speak to her about the great yeshivahs, rabbis, and men of letters in other towns and cities, she would listen in rapt silence. It was then that she decided to spend her life in study, devoting her every thought to Talmudic inquiry and disputation. She loved to reason by dialogue, to investigate abstract notions, to weigh many possibilities in an attempt to discern certain truths. Exposition, discussion, systematic reasoning, and the juxtaposition of ideas triggered by a plethora of questions and answers excited her. Such thought-provoking interaction, leading so frequently to theoretical application of mental constructs, absorbed her every minute.

Yentl was "obstinate." Despite the peer pressure applied to her following her father's death, she sold her house and furniture, willingly incurring a loss in so doing. She cut her braids, careful to keep enough hair for sidelocks at her temples, then donned her father's clothes. Placing her phylacteries, some books, and her own underclothes in a small basket that she would carry with her, Yentl left Yanev at night in the month of Av (May), with 140 rubles to her name. That her departure took place in the fifth month of the Jewish year may in part refer to God, the Divine Father (*av*), who comforted Himself in the month of Av, 587 B.C.E. after Nebuchadnezzar destroyed the temple that Solomon had built in His honor. Soon the Jews would be led away from Jerusalem into exile in Nebuchadnezzar's Babylonia. Yentl, too, would leave the warmth and security of a family existence that was no more as she set out on her journey into the unknown.

Yentl went to Lublin on foot. For both intellectual and psychological reasons, that this city was once the home of Meir Ben Gedaliah (1558–1616), the famous and much admired codifier and commentator of the Talmud, may have been instrumental in dictating her choice.

Father Identification

Yentl's strong father identification implied a rejection of what she considered to be the empty life led by the women of her community who devoted themselves exclusively to child rearing, cooking, idle conversation, and ignorance. Opting for the opposite extreme, Yentl was determined, no matter the cost, to live a life of the mind.

Although she was unaware of its ramifications, uppermost in Yentl's thinking was her repudiation of a way of life prevailing in many ultrapatriarchal societies in Eastern Europe. Not only were women imprisoned in their anatomy; even more contemptible, they were considered unworthy and unfit for advanced religious study, as previously mentioned. Although cognizant to a certain extent of the anatomical differences between the sexes, Yentl rejected taboos and regulations dictating the activities of females. The melding of cultural and religious values in an attempt to relegate women to subordinate positions, particularly in questions of education, was anathema to Yentl. Because she understood that her community would not transcend sexual differences, she would be obliged to resort to her own devices to deconstruct gender prohibitions. In time, she hoped that androcentric values would either diminish or vanish (Reis 1991, p. 26). Yentl's father identification, to a great extent, worked positively for her. It gave her the necessary support and self-confidence to further her ideological struggle.

Let us examine some of the inequities involved in the social structure of Yentl's era and group. While elementary education for male children was compulsory from the ages of 4 to 13, girls were simply taught their prayers, and if they did know how to read, their learning consisted mostly of Yiddish translations of the Bible. There were, to be sure, some exceptions: women whose husbands spent their lives in study and prayer yielded the burden of money-earning to their wives.

The curriculum for boys studying in community schools (*heders*) focused, for the most part, on religious studies: the Talmud and rabbinics. Poverty was so great in many communities that conditions in some schools, frequently limited to a single room in the teacher's home, were appallingly inadequate. The following is a description of a *heder* in Vitebsk in 1894:

> Our Talmud Torahs are filthy rooms, crowded from nine in the morning until nine in the evening with pale, starved children. These remain in this contaminated atmosphere for twelve hours at a time and see only their bent, exhausted teachers. . . . Most of them are clad in rags; some of them are almost naked. . . . Their faces are pale and sickly, and their bodies are evidently not strong. In parties of twenty or thirty, and at times more, they all repeat some lesson aloud after their instructor. He who has not listened to the almost absurd commentaries of the ignorant melammed [teacher] cannot even imagine how little the children gain from such instruction. (Baron 1942, p. 142)

The unsatisfactory conditions prevailing in so many schools did not deter serious adolescents from pursuing their studies. On the contrary, in many instances, it fired their enthusiasm. From the *heder* they went to the *yeshivah* (seminary). Many continued their education even after marriage. Religious study for these young men became a way of life, explaining perhaps the high rate of literacy in Jewish communities as compared to the low rate among their Christian neighbors.

The reputation of yeshivahs, directed frequently by prestigious rabbis, grew in keeping with the number of advanced students attending. Since budgets were limited, the community, intent upon insuring the tradition of learning, supported and even endowed these institutions. It was the custom for poor students to be sent on specific days to take their meals at the homes of wealthier members of the community. Although the poverty of teachers and students was great, learning was so significant a factor in their lives that they were not only devoted to their studies, but also took pride in their individual houses of learning, where they believed they were fulfilling "Judaism's supreme commandment" (Baron 1942, p. 142).

Because Yentl had been nurtured in the belief that education was sacred, she would, understandably, identify with its values and with those who furthered this discipline. Moreover, hadn't the importance of education been emphasized since biblical times? In Deuteronomy we read: "Thou shalt teach them diligently unto the children" (6:7). Hadn't the scribe Ezra, upon his return to Jerusalem in 458 B.C.E. from his people's enforced exile in Babylonia, been empowered by the victorious Persian king Artaxerxes to institute regular public readings of the Torah? Indeed, Simeon Ben Shetah (1st century B.C.E.) is known to have lain the foundations for standards of local elementary and higher level schools which became the prototype of Jewish communal education for centuries to come.

Why were the Torah, the Talmud (Hebrew, "teaching"), and commentaries taught and studied so assiduously in Hebrew schools? What was it about these books that had motivated Yentl not only intellectually but emotionally as well?

The Torah (the Pentateuch, or the first five books of Moses: Genesis, Exodus, Leviticus, Numbers, Deuteronomy) consists of both written law and oral law. The former, involving the teachings given by God to Moses on Mt. Sinai, were recorded: "And the Lord said unto Moses, Write thou these words: for after the tenor of these words I have made a covenant with thee and with Israel" (Exodus 34:27). To Joshua, Divinity spoke as follows: "This book of the law shall not depart out of thy mouth, but thou shalt meditate therein day and night" (Joshua 1:8). The ancient rabbis believed this injunction to mean that one must devote one's entire life to the study of the

Torah. The oral law, on the other hand, was given to Moses by divine revelation and was not written down, but rather transmitted by oral tradition.

The Talmud, a unique religious and literary work, includes legal and nonlegal material: legends, folklore, ethical, philosophical, theosophical, and theological speculations, parables, prayers, homilies, gnomic sayings, historical reminiscences, etc. Its content is a composite of studies and discussions by scholars in the academies throughout Palestine and Babylonia from approximately 30 B.C.E. to 500 C.E. For centuries scholars had interpreted the written law in keeping with the specific admonitions, cases, and opinions of the various teachers and individual schools prior to the destruction of the Second Temple (70 C.E.) by Titus.

The oral law—the explanatory part of divine revelation, which was not recorded in the Pentateuch—although imparted to Moses on Mt. Sinai, was committed to writing by Judah the Prince (2nd century C.E.) in the Mishnah ("repetition" and "learning"). A kind of textbook, the Mishnah was made up of interpretations, discussions, and disputations of the oral law as understood by sages since Mosaic times. So many different and conflicting opinions of oral law had been handed down by scholars from one generation to the next that Judah the Prince decided to compile in book form the masses of information accepted by tradition. In that the Mishnah did not reveal all the reasons accounting for the opinions and verdicts offered by the scholars—and perhaps purposefully so—it was up to the students reading these injunctions and disputations to discover the meanings for themselves. In so doing, they would not only be refining and sharpening their own thought processes, but would be completing what was lacking in their understanding of religious doctrine. The second part of the Talmud, the Gemara ("completion"), not only offers discussions and analyses relating to each part of each case included in the Mishnah, but also sets out to compare the similarities between them and, unlike the Mishnah, arrives at a conclusion. The Gemara also comprises commentaries and deliberations bearing on historical figures, scriptural texts, and many aspects of daily existence (Kravitz 1972, p. 145).

The Mishnah, a fascinating kind of reference work, is also imbued with poetry and history, yielding the essence of the oral law transmitted by the wisest of the wise since Mosaic times. Absorbing as well as challenging, the interaction of the ideas enunciated involves a system of questions and answers as well as analogical and associative techniques as a basis for the discussions. Such a thinking mode is incredibly varied in subject matter and in range. The goal of the mental gymnastics indulged in by such ancient sages as the rabbis Hillel, Akiva, Meir, and Johanan in constituting or creating the Mishnah and Gemara was not merely for educational, legal, or cerebral purposes. The driving force behind the disputations and ideological discussions carried on throughout the centuries and then committed to writing was the participants' way of discovering—at least partially—the essential truth of things. Rather than underscoring or encouraging divisiveness of opinions and principles in their nuanced disputations, and instead of separating groups and triggering schisms, an attempt was made to discern affinities between the participants and their ideas, thus bringing the disparate together. The subtlety and logic of the finely tuned Talmudic arguments led scholars on many an occasion to come upon flaws in their own inquiries, which enabled them to rectify their arguments and judgments.

Like the scientist and the mathematician, the Talmudist, or pursuer of truth, had to exercise precision in measuring his ideas and weighing his views. Only in this manner could he begin to flesh out the word of God, or absolute truth. Because the Talmud was built layer upon layer, each generation becoming both receiver and imparter of knowledge, those engaging in the study and scrutiny of everything concerning the Torah and all that followed were participating in a creative endeavor as well as a religious one (Steinsaltz 1986, pp. 2–6).

The Ten Commandments, as given by God to Moses on Mt. Sinai, although comprising only ten sentences, resulted in an enormous compendium of laws—"A Torah of Life." That so much written matter had been elicited by the religious event is explained as follows in the Talmud (Berakhoth 2): "Whatever a well-versed student of the Torah might ever expound had been given already to Moses on Mount Sinai" (Kravitz 1972, p. 145). Since all information is believed to exist in the Torah, it is incumbent upon the student to detect, in blessedness as well as in awe, the proper interpretation of the hidden aspects of this sacred work.

For Yentl, her father, and for the male community at large, the Talmudic world was a living expression of human joys and agonies, intellectual constructs and intuitive imagings. It comes as no surprise that everything connected with the Mishnah and the Gemara absorbed Yentl's entire world. The aura and mystery surrounding the names of such great sages as Rabbi Hillel (1st century B.C.E.) and Rabbi Akiva (40–135 C.E.) may have been a factor in arousing Yentl's fascination. What was of essential import to her, however, was the line of the argument undertaken and the nature of each individual's reasoning powers. Right thinking, the sages repeated always, paved the way for *right action*, the latter being more important than the former (Goldin 1957, pp. 14–15).

The Talmud—thanks to Yentl's father—opened up a world of abstraction to her. She seemed to thrive on the tensions the contradictory ideologies triggered in her mind and psyche as well as the intellectual processes used to resolve them. To participate in such highly tuned dialectics harmonized with her personality. Awed by the diversity of the subjects pondered by past scholars as well as by the movement of their minds as they flowed and sometimes jumped from theme to theme awaiting or intuiting new insights catalyzed by old ones, she was invited to experience the numinous. Thanks to her own talents, developed and heightened by her father's daily lessons, the logic of Yentl's contentions, the sharpness of her analyses, and the sensitivity of her interpretations of scriptural exegesis developed, tested, and strengthened her mental faculties.

The Thinking Type

Yentl's father, a dispenser of wisdom, had been a man of the Word and of the Book. Judging from his lifestyle, he believed that God, YHWH, omnipresent and invisible, revealed His presence and His creative power through the Word. In Genesis, for example, we read that "God *said*, let there be light . . . And God *said*, Let there be a firmament in the midst of the waters . . ." etc. (Genesis 1:3,6). It was via the word/breath that the world came into being. Yentl's identification with her father had been and still was so strong that she, too, experienced intellectual and spiritual renewal through auditory mentation.

Not the image of God, whose representation was prohibited in Hebrew tradition to avoid regressing into idol worship, but rather the Word in His Voice, was forever present in the Hebrew's psyche. Isaiah, for example, wrote of the numinous experience he had had when hearing the voice of God in the temple: "A voice of noise from the city, a voice from the temple, a voice of the Lord . . ." (Isaiah 66:6). Voice lived potently within Yentl's obscurity.

A hypostatized animus figure—a master of wisdom, protector, guide, and inspiration—not only functioned archetypally in Yentl's psyche in the form of Divinity, but throughout her young life was supplemented by the voice and presence of her *personal* father. The concept of the Wise Old Man, constellated both archetypally and personally, gave her access to the libido, or psychic energy, necessary to help shape and define her future. In that the presence of this spiritual macro and micro Wise Old Man force emerged from the deepest sources of her unconscious, it was transformed, in keeping with her typology, into logos. As such, divine speech, the creative word, and the thinking process in general became a mediating principle between God/Father and Yentl. Indeed, it became her *raison d'être*.

Because of this harmonious tripartite relationship, Yentl had no regrets, no guilt feelings, no psychological problem in selling her house and her belongings and leaving the town in which she had spent all of her days. On the contrary, she understood, perhaps instinctively, that to remain in a community where she was known and where she would have to fight the status quo openly would have negative ramifications. Or, if she were to yield to marriage and a life inimicable to her yearnings, she would be relegated to the home, which she considered a stifling, if not deadly lifestyle. Moreover, in the latter case, she would most probably have only a most superficial relationship with her husband. Had it not been stated that any serious student of the Talmud should not indulge in idle chatter with women, even with his own wife? In the words of Maimonides:

> It is a known thing that for the most part conversation with women has to do with sexual matters. That is why Yose ben Johanan says that much talk with them is forbidden, for by such talk a man brings evil upon himself. (Goldin 1957, p. 55)

Students of the Talmud were advised to acquire a male friend with whom to converse and study scripture, "and reveal to him all his secrets, the secrets of the Torah and the secrets of worldly things" (ibid., pp. 55, 57).

Yentl was certain that even though she was not male, she had made the right choice. There could be no other way but to devote her life to study and thoughtful discussion. Had it not been written in the Mishnah:

For so long as words of the Torah enter and find the chambers of the heart unoccupied, they make their home in the person—and the evil impulse can have no dominion over him and no one can drive away these words from him. A parable is told: to what may this be likened? To a king who was on a journey; he came upon a palace whose rooms were unoccupied, and entered and occupied them. No man can expel him from there. So too, so long as the words of the Torah upon entering find the chambers of the heart unoccupied, they make their home in it; the evil impulse can have no dominion there and no one can drive these words away. (Ibid., p. 51)

Rather than experiencing a void after her father's death, Yentl felt strong enough to make the transition from passive to active learning. In this manner, she was certain she would not only enrich her understanding of the written text but deepen her knowledge of spiritual matters by questioning, supposing, and receiving clarification of elements beyond her ken. She was also aware of the fact that now that her father was gone she would have to search for a master or teacher capable of enlightening her with regard to new concepts, precise argumentation, and consistency in her disputations while also inviting her to fathom the moral and theological implications of the suppositions under scrutiny.

Study, for a thinking type such as Yentl, was the main source of her nourishment. Because mentation had been awakened under her father's tutelage, she considered herself certainly equal if not superior to others of her age, at least in analytical matters. In terms of empirical experience, however, because she knew so little about the outside world, she was oblivious to the obstacles that might beset her once she left the security of her home environment. She did understand that, in moving from a cloistered existence into the external world, she would be unable to adhere to the strict religious laws and prohibitions regarding her sex. Henceforth, her behavior would adhere to a pattern of gender deception.

Because her father had both loved and respected Yentl for her mental capabilities, he had inculcated in her feelings of self-worth. The archetypal pattern that had been set since her earliest days had served not only to activate her libido but to fix such concepts as learning—a Godly undertaking—as primordial. She minimized the difficulties, gender related or not, that might present themselves in the pursuit of her goal. Such a positive and energetic approach to life had also been instrumental in Yentl's acceptance of her father's death as a fact of life. Rather than spending her days lamenting his demise and the void it left in her world, she looked forward to fulfilling herself as a scholar, thus following in his footsteps or recreating his image in herself. In so doing, she was in fact obeying, rather than defying, both her father's way and her own nature.

The "soul of a man" which her father had discerned in Yentl helped her to deal with and adapt to each new problem as it arose (Harding 1973, p. 57). The direction taken by her thoughts, emerging as they did from unconscious roots, divested her of any conflict between her judgmental faculties and her conscious objective. Perhaps such mental mechanisms posed a problem of which she was unaware: she was not sufficiently cognizant of the possible ramifications of her acts or statements. Because Yentl's rational function was forever arranging possibilities and formulating suppositions in accordance with her subjective needs, she overlooked and therefore remained untroubled by a fundamental *untruth*: her comportment. The fact that she would be posing as a man, thereby resorting to distortion, thus disobeying the Talmud's interdict, seemed not to bother her in the slightest. If any problem concerning her gender were to arise, she felt, her reasoning powers would always be on the alert to quell any stressful thought that might arise.

Because Yentl's forte was abstraction, her perception and cognition, when focused on Talmudic matters, were objective and evidently worked wonderfully well since she earned the admiration of her father. As defined by Jung:

> Abstraction . . . is a form of mental activity that frees this content from its associations with the irrelevant elements by distinguishing it from them, or, in other words, *differentiating* it. (Jung 1971, par. 677)

Yentl's propensity for abstraction had developed her rational function to the extreme. Through conceptualization she had learned how to separate, differentiate, and distinguish one theme or idea from the whole. A world revolving around such mental feats required isolation on her part: the divestiture of everything that was not connected with her projected goal. Thus, she was cut off from her feeling function and further removed from the world of reality. Because she identified exclusively with books, thinking, and disputation, the question arises as to whether she risked being swallowed up by her excessive needs.

Until her departure from her hometown, her thinking was so well regulated that it held her inferior feeling function in check. Under stressful conditions, however, would her conscious attitude always be capable of weighing the full value or impact of the objective conditions at hand? Would her actions always be based on an impartial and impersonal examination of the entire scheme of things and all factors involved? Or, on the contrary, might she condition them subjectively (ibid., pars. 830–833)? The fact that she did not fully consider, prior to acting, those things that remained outside of her realm of experience might, at least in part, account for the painful events to follow.

Persona

Yentl considered it crucial to wear her father's clothes. Only under such a disguise could she cope with—in her way, challenge—the conventional society in which she lived. By so doing, however, she was putting on a male persona, or social face. Unlike the ruling figure in Andersen's fairy tale, "The Emperor's New Clothes," Yentl was very much aware of hiding the naked truth. Only under a disguise would she be able to function as she wished and without earning castigation. At least, this is what she believed.

Yentl's clothes represented a secret attitude, enclosing her in the dark or the unconscious. Let us recall that her father had always drawn the curtains before they began studying the Talmud. Yentl is resorting to a similar device—deception—in order to protect her treasure: logos. Indeed, wasn't she merely following her father's example (von Franz 1974, pp. 21–22)?

When adherence to ethics, morality, and traditional rules of behavior—prerequisite and, therefore, *essential* to Talmudic study—is transgressed, a serious breach has been committed. Ingenuity, rather than truth, had been made available to Yentl by her father's example. Her own well-developed cognitive sense simply took it a step further. Were she to have probed spiritual paths as she had legal questions, she would have realized that by circumventing the very fabric of Judaic rules of behavior, she was blaspheming. Grave dangers lie ahead for those taking such a route. To step beyond what is considered a respectful attitude toward one's co-religionists required enormous inner drive on her part, as well as a finely tuned and well-equipped mind able to see clear amid the complex twistings and turnings of casuistic demarcations. Yentl was endowed with both.

Unlike Job, who laid bare his heart, Yentl resorted to an interplay of right and wrong to gain her ends. By drawing a veil over her physical being she would be allowed the freedom to develop her mental pursuits in the name of God. The lowering of her ethical values had not even come into question. Living in the world of the mind as she did, she was convinced that she was serving God in her own special way. And perhaps she was! That her personal moral code did not coincide with what she considered to be intransigent collective obligations in no way discouraged her zest to reach her goal nor diminished her self-confidence. Because she believed God to be with her, she felt capable of fulfilling her innermost ideal. The numinosity of her religious experience imbued her with a strange sensation of certainty.

A Collision Course

Conceptual approaches via the word-and-thought complex as adumbrated in the Talmud had always been Yentl's daily fare as well as her daily challenge. Such mental meanderings invited her to draw upon conventional and nontraditional explications and interpretations when arguing the multiple meanings of scriptural content. The stimulation provided by the Talmud, with its analyses, interpretations, explications, and hermeneutical approaches to every phase of existence, enveloped her very being. Her world was *aflame*. In Exodus, however, we are warned:

> If fire break out, and catch in thorns, so that the stack of corn, or the standing corn, or the field, be consumed therewith; he that kindled the fire shall surely make restitution. (Exodus 22:6)

A price must paid whenever an inner flame breaks out of its protective sheath. Yentl's desire to become a "Man of the Book" would not free her from her ordeal.

Let us recall that Yentl left her hometown at night, when everyone was asleep. A strong ego (center of consciousness) had motivated her to leave the safety of a community, to go against the collective code, and to indulge in deception. Yentl, in this area, was no different from many a young hero, a Siegfried or a Parzival, starting out on his great quest. Naive, lacking in judgment and experience, and devoid of sophistication, they were not cognizant of fear as they forged ahead in their search for a new spiritual life.

Yentl, unlike Siegfried and Parzival, had been well grounded. Her study of the Talmud was not only a record of a mental, spiritual, and psychological process but was a living monument of her ability to partake in the intellectual food it offered. It was a measure, to some extent, of her own spiritual and intellectual evolution. After feasting with the greats of all time, how could anything in the mundane world generate in Yentl anything but boredom? But because she was so cut off from the world of reality, obstacles and trials would beset her, as they had so many heroes of the past, in order to rectify a blatant imbalance in the psyche. The problems and stressful circumstances she would have to face may be viewed as tests intended to develop her discretionary faculties and deepen her ethical understanding.

The agonizing choices of the biblical Deborah, let us recall, also led her on a collision course. Although she was a judge and a prophetess who had "dwelt under the palm tree" waiting "for the children of Israel to come up to her for judgment," she took an extraordinarily hazardous stand when, in God's name, she requested that the warrior Barak liberate the Hebrews from domination by King Jabin of Hazor (Judges 4:5).[1] Because of her evidently well developed and harmonious thinking and feeling functions, she was prepared to compromise with Barak when he demanded that she accompany him in his military campaign: "If thou wilt go with me, then I will go: but if thou wilt not go with me, then I will not go" (Judges 4:8). After acquiescing to his terms, she replied by posing her own. She let Barak know that he was to expect no sexual favors from her: "notwithstanding the journey that thou takest shall not be for thine honour . . ." (Judges 4:9). In so doing, she fought the sexism prevalent in the society of her day. She was her own person, openly and vehemently.

Like Deborah, Yentl would also have to fight her own war, not only with regard to the outside world, but even more seriously in terms of her own inner attitude based on ethical values and a whole repressed feeling domain. She would likewise have to learn the meaning of conciliation and malleability along the way.

The Main Road

Once Yentl reached the main road after leaving her hometown, she was offered a ride to Zamosc, after which she walked on alone until she reached an inn. There she met other students en route to study with famous rabbis. She listened attentively to their discussions, centering for the most part on the greatness of some yeshivahs in Lithuania and Poland as opposed to others. Since she had never been in the company of young men before, although impressed by the tenor of their conversations, Yentl did not join in, fearing perhaps that she might say the wrong thing. No sooner had the conversations taken a less serious turn than one of the young men poked her on the shoulder and asked: "Why so quiet? Don't you have a tongue?" After she replied by telling him she had nothing to say, he tweaked her nose. Although angered by his words and gesture, she restrained herself. Meanwhile, Avigdor, a slightly older student, "tall and pale, with burning eyes and a black beard, came to her rescue."

Yentl, now calling herself Anshel, after a dead uncle, warmed to Avigdor's thoughtful and understanding ways. When she told him she was looking for a quiet yeshivah, he suggested she come with him to Bechev. There she could study with the head of his religious academy who was, in his words, a "genius." So brilliant was he, that "he could pose ten questions and answer all ten with one proof." Added incentives: the yeshivah was small, with only thirty students attending; the families in the town provided the students with food and took care of their laundry and sewing; last, most of the students found wives in the community.

Avigdor explained to Yentl/Anshel that because his mother had died in the middle of the last term, he had left the yeshivah and was now returning to complete his studies. When Yentl/Anshel asked him why he was not married, he told her he had been in love with and engaged to Hadass, the only daughter of Alter Vishkower, the wealthiest man in town. For no apparent reason their engagement had been broken. Since that incident, he had turned down other suggestions offered him by marriage brokers. (Later he learned that his engagement had been called off because his brother had committed suicide.) Tense, shy, perhaps embarrassed at his ill luck, "behind [Avigdor's] high furrowed brow his thoughts seemed to race." Annoyed perhaps for having disclosed such intimate details to a stranger, he spoke defensively: "Well, what of it. I'll become a recluse, that's all."

Was it an example of synchronicity that Yentl/Anshel should have been the one to be sent to Hadass's home for her weekly meals? When an outer happening seems to coincide in a meaningful way with an inner psychological condition, it may be said that an unconscious identification has occurred between the individual and the external world. Such a phenomenon, Jung suggested, brings a "border zone" into being, in which contents from conscious and subliminal spheres contiguous to each other flow into one another, thereby triggering an *abaissement du niveau mental*. In that the unconscious exists in a space-time continuum, it functions in a fourth dimension, thereby eliminating such three-dimensional notions as past, present, future, causality, and space differentiation (Jacobi 1959, pp. 62–3).

The coincidental happening of seemingly unrelated events experienced by Yentl/Anshel not only had meaning for her but may have been viewed by her as an *a priori* fact: derived by reasoning from self-evident propositions. Such a deductive premise was perfectly logical for a thinking type. The synchronistic event did not appear incompatible with Yentl/Anshel's strong ego, which seemed, at this juncture, to be in harmony with the Self, or total psyche. Jung defines the Self not only as containing the deposit and totality of all past life but as a point of departure, the fertile soil from which all future life will spring. This premonition of futurity is as clearly impressed upon our innermost feelings as the historical aspect. The idea of immortality follows legitimately from these psychological premises (Jacobi 1959, p. 65).

Yentl/Anshel's access to archetypal levels, and the unfortunate contamination that could emerge between subliminal and rational spheres, might not necessarily work in her favor in human relationships or in life situations. For the time being, however, things seemed to be going well. Since the students at the yeshivah studied in pairs, she and Avigdor, soon on friendly terms, chose each other. Not only did he help her with her studies but invited her to share his lodgings. For obvious reasons, Yentl/Anshel chose to live with an aged and nearly blind widow. During their study periods together, however, Avigdor always questioned his new friend about Hadass. How did she look? Was a marriage being planned for her? Yentl/Anshel's answers were so perfunctory that he concluded that Hadass did not appeal to his study partner.

So fond did Yentl/Anshel become of Avigdor that to show her feeling for him she began buying him presents: a silk handkerchief, a scarf, etc. He in turn felt so much affection for Yentl/Anshel that he even suggested that his friend marry Hadass. "Never," she replied. Some time later, Avigdor informed Yentl/Anshel that he had accepted the matchmaker's offer to marry the wealthy widow

Peshe. Although the widow was the owner of a herring, tar, pot, and pan shop, Yentl/Anshel advised him against such a plan. She is cowlike: neither clever nor pretty, and because her husband had died during the first year of their marriage, she is to be typed as a husband-killer. He agreed, but much embarrassed, he confessed, "I need a woman. I can't sleep at night." Startled by such an admission, Yentl/Anshel asked him why he could not wait for the right girl to respond. Avigdor became engaged to Peshe and, predictably, his problems began, as did Yentl/Anshel's.

Because the weeks prior to Avigdor's marriage were taken up with material concerns such as outfitting the groom, the head of the yeshivah asked Yentl/Anshel to choose another study partner. No one, she told herself, could begin to take Avigdor's place, spiritually or intellectually. Indeed, "without Avigdor the study house seemed empty." At night, alone in her room, after having removed her men's clothes, she was once again a woman—and a woman in love. "Perhaps I should have told him the truth?" she thought. On the other hand, now that she had been indoctrinated into the world of books and study, she realized she could not possibly turn back the clock and live like a girl. Disturbed by her first great conflictual episode, Yentl/Anshel believed herself close to madness.

Although warm and authentic, Yentl was so introverted and her feeling function so primitive that when it was a question of human relationships she seemed to lose all ability to judge or calculate. Had she been capable of assessing her feelings objectively, she might have better understood the risks at stake: including losing sight of life.

The Dream

So intense was Yentl/Anshel's dilemma that she awakened from a dream one night with a start. "In her dream she had been at the same time a man and a woman, wearing both a woman's bodice and a man's fringed garment." Even more emotionally assaulting on her than her dream was the real life fact: the lateness of her menstrual cycle. She feared the worst, and understandably. Had the Talmud (*Medrash Talpioth*) not told of the plight of a woman who had conceived simply by desiring a man? For the first time, she understood why the Torah prohibits wearing the clothing of a person of the other sex. Such deception served to confuse not only society but the individual as well. "Even the soul was perplexed," she thought, upon "finding itself incarnate in a strange body."

Clearly, Yentl/Anshel's rational domain was no longer in command. Nor could study, once her main food and that healthy sustaining factor in her psyche, come to her rescue. Her archetypal dream had pointed to the schism between the persona that she had so cavalierly donned and what lay hidden beneath the mask: the woman. The two not only did not fit together any longer but had become incompatible with one another. Even more significant was the possibility of a takeover by her inferior feeling function. No longer would she be reasoning her way out of unpleasant or difficult situations. Instead, the woman in love would be directing the way. Slowly, but incisively, her manly mask was corroding, obliterating that self-confidence, that joy she had formerly experienced during her many intellectual disputations with Avigdor. How could anything but psychological dismemberment follow? Yentl/Anshel found herself unable to eat, study, or even talk. So dissociated and intertwined had her two personalities become that one overflowed into the other.

Where would her next step take her? The environment Yentl/Anshel had chosen to inhabit required her to maintain her persona at all times. If outer factors had not intervened to upset the delicate balance, such a disjunctive situation could perhaps have prevailed. On the other hand, when an individual is deeply stressed, as Yentl/Anshel was, unsettling results cannot help but intrude. Because her persona, identified with a conscious intent, was being perpetually bombarded by upsurges of feeling tones emanating from her subliminal sphere, the dichotomy between the increasingly disjointed facets of her inner and outer personalities invited chaos. Alone, with no one to share her secret, she failed to understand how to deal with the inner stirrings leaping about within her. Each claimed autonomy over the other; each took possession of her at different moments. Unrelated to herself as well as to her milieu, she felt tyrannized by the emotions her thinking function failed to understand. Longing for truth, relatedness, and love, her feeling world was at odds with the rational construct she had created for herself in order to carry out her life's goal. The two polarities broadened, bringing into being what Jung called a condition of *enantiodromia*. The friction between these extremes served to activate unconscious contents, which became manifest in her archetypal dream.

The gender confusion projected in her dream colored Yentl/Anshel's whole existence. Life, so exciting and fruitful a force prior to the broadening of her inner schism, had taken on a negative cast. Gloom, fear, and an abrasive view of her existential sphere haunted her every thought. No longer independent, she had become increasingly impressionable, her former strength becoming a weakness. The once intellectual persona was yielding to the emotional, sentimental, and tender woman beneath.

That Yentl/Anshel found herself unable to eat or even function in the real world indicated the immediacy of her stressful situation. Her libido, channeled so successfully prior to Avigdor's engagement, could no longer be dammed up. It exploded with such power that her thinking process shriveled. Incredibly, therefore, when Yentl/Anshel next visited Hadass, she asked the young lady to become her wife. Only after uttering her marriage proposal did she begin to understand the depth of her entanglement "in evil." Why had she spoken as she had? she wondered, concluding that it was some power within her that "kept urging her on."

The Autonomous Complex

Yentl/Anshel's emotional development had not kept pace with her mental growth. Because ancient or traditional attitudes simply do not fade away even if new needs emerge, the powers within her could no longer contain the increasingly demanding polarities inhabiting her psyche. The energy centers or nuclei of fiery essences making up these warring extremes had displaced and fragmented what had been her formerly smooth-running thinking function.

Yentl/Anshel's error was in part brought on by her undervaluation of her feeling world. Overly hungry for knowledge, as Faust had been prior to the onset of his initiatory journey, she had been unaware of how much she yearned for relatedness and more importantly, for love. She had advanced her thinking function at the expense of a whole underdeveloped feeling domain associated, unfortunately, only with the feminine. In so doing, she became inflated, considering herself superior to women in general: "With girls I can play as I please!" Wasn't Yentl/Anshel, then, unconsciously attempting to destroy what she considered inferior, that is, her own feminine feeling side? Hadn't she, moments after proposing to Hadass, gasped and said: "What have I done? I must be going mad." Only later did she realize that Avigdor had been the one who had wanted to marry Hadass and not she. So disconnected had

Yentl/Anshel become that she had identified with Avigdor. Not only had she lost sight of her own identity, but had unconsciously proclaimed herself Avigdor's self-appointed guardian capable of fulfilling his desires.

Suffering most frequently lies ahead for the person whose ego has not only arrogated unto itself what is not properly within its dominion but has become so inflated as to lead an individual out of the world of reality. As psychopomp, Yentl's ego had so altered her mode of behavior as to direct her actions and thoughts into borderline channels. Such steps led to her rebellion against the social and ethical conventions of her religious upbringing.

In a well-adjusted person, the ego is made up of many complexes—that is, groups of ideas pertaining to the ego. This ego complex, as it is termed, is able to cope with most problems relating to the individual and is considered "the highest psychic unity of authority" (Jung 1960, par. 82). When disturbed, however, the psychic totality may become fragmented and split up into various complexes. When such a splitting off occurs, each complex may be looked upon as a kind of miniature self-contained psyche which develops a peculiar fantasy life of its own (ibid., pars. 59, 90). Under such circumstances, a complex may become virtually autonomous, as occurred in Yentl/Anshel's case, the resulting fantasies assuming abnormal proportions. Autonomous complexes may be looked upon as toxins because they do not fit into the conscious mind harmoniously and may resist all attempts on the part of the will to cope with them. Complexes are endowed with a type of electric current; they possess affective charges and feeling tones. The affects given off by a complex are sometimes so great as to be capable of acting physically upon the person experiencing the complex. Respiration, blood pressure, the circulatory system may all be altered, depending upon the power of the complex over the individual. Let us recall, in this regard, that Yentl/Anshel could neither eat, sleep, nor talk. When certain exceptionally deep-rooted complexes break through into consciousness, they can erupt with such extreme violence that they invade the entire personality. Such an explosive condition had led Yentl/Anshel to propose marriage to Hadass.

Although Yentl/Anshel had no evil intent in asking for Hadass's hand, by doing so, she had showed herself to be completely cut off from reality. Rather than integrating the split-off content, the autonomous psychic complex had gone its own way, inviting her to transgress *all* ethical and moral rules of behavior. Disrespectful of all decorum, these unredeemed packets of energy had, on the contrary, encouraged her to step over the borderline of acceptable and accountable modes of behavior: her shadow prevailed.

Whether identified with the shadow, evil, or Satan, that power within Yentl/Anshel which, she claimed, "kept urging her on," dominated her rational sphere. A whole secret, negative, and devilish world was fomenting within this formerly noble girl who had once set out to rectify a weak link in collective thinking. Because she had hitherto known only paternal and Godly affection and never those catalytic emotions inspired by love between man and woman, she was unable to shackle these unbridled powers. Although seeking to go her way, as Job had, unlike the biblical figure she had not lain her heart bare. She had merely drawn a curtain over that living and earthly part of her personality. Mistakenly, she thought that by wearing man's clothing and applying her mind to manly studies she would succeed in blocking out and even destroying the woman beneath. The opposite occurred: the passionate feeling force repressed for so long had been transformed into a deeply demanding power.

Irrationally, Yentl/Anshel forged ahead. So inflated and distended had her ego become, so blind to its own limitations, that it felt ready to take on the whole world. "The public are fools," she mused. Her projected marriage to Hadass encouraged her to say to herself: "Now I'll really start something." Because her entire psyche had fallen under the dominion of her complex, everything she did, thought, and felt centered around her distorted views. Balance had been lost. As the complex gained in strength and vigor, the rest of the psyche starved and atrophied. Events and statements in her daily life not pertaining in some way to her complex were sloughed off whereas relatively insignificant statements or acts that she felt were related to her complex became all-important. As the day of Avigdor's impending marriage approached, Yentl/Anshel began suffering other physical symptoms besides inability to eat or speak: she could not sleep, her throat was parched, her forehead feverish, her knees weak, and her stomach began playing tricks on her. "A quarrel seemed to be going on inside her. It was as if she had sealed a pact with Satan, the Evil One who plays tricks on human beings, who sets stumbling blocks and traps in their path." So distraught had she become that she spent her days in the study house, hoping to find some help in the patriarchal sphere of law, dogma, order, and knowledge.

Satan: *Spiritus Agens* of Change

Had Satan really entered her being? Had Satan been the one to involve her more deeply and virtually inextricably in a blasphemous situation? Before exploring these questions, let us first examine Satan's place in Hebrew religious thought.

Because the Hebrew God is suprapersonal, infinite, and immanent, He incorporates All, including the empirical concepts of good and evil. Exodus acquaints us with Divinity's thirteen attributes: love and hate, kindness and punishment, etc. (Exodus 34:5–7). God for the Hebrew, then, is a composite of opposites. In Deuteronomy, He states: "See, I have set before thee this day life and good, and death and evil" (30:15). In Isaiah, we read: "I form the light, and create darkness: I make peace, and create evil: I the Lord do all these things" (45:7). Unlike the Hebrews, the Christians conceive of Christ as all good (all light, all spirit), thereby rejecting the notion of evil as implicit in Him and relegating it to the Antichrist.

In Judaism, evil (or anything connected with this cosmic power, such as demonic spirits, which were creatures of the Lord and thus part of Him) was and is part of Divinity. In Deuteronomy, it is stated: "thou mightest know that the Lord He is God; there is none else beside him" (4:35). Under the influence of Persian and Hellenistic schools of thought, the concept of evil became concretized in Satan, Belial, and Beelzebub. As the son of God, Satan was the "adversary," the "accuser," the one to inject feelings of suspicion into Job, among others, thus becoming instrumental in his suffering. In this regard, Satan was both finite and infinite: finite in his malevolent attitude toward Job, and infinite as a negative principle in God Himself. The confrontation that took place among the three forces involved—Job, Satan, and God—may be conceived as a concretization of antagonistic principles within the Godhead (Kluger 1967, p. 52).

Blaming her malaise on Satan, the adversary within her, was Yentl/Anshel's way of explaining away the inner antagonism invading her world. Satan was indeed that power that incited her to go ahead with her plan and marry Hadass. It was he who disturbed her peace of mind, thereby upsetting the smooth-running rational plan she had mapped out for herself upon leaving her hometown. As an aspect of God (psychologically, the Self), he had been sent to hinder and obstruct, thereby to activate contents in Yentl/Anshel's unconscious. Only after experiencing such spiritual and physical malaise would she begin to clarify and then rectify the deception she was perpetrating with regard to others and to herself. Satan, in Yentl/Anshel's case, may be considered to be a hypostatized or personified divine function of "opposition," a demon ready to confront her dialectically on her own turf and force her to examine at greater length her deeply manipulative stand (Kluger 1967, p. 40).

One might question Satan's timing. Why had he chosen to manifest himself at this point in Yentl's development? Evidently, it corresponded to a need to make conscious what had not thus far been expressed. By allowing that Satanic or colliding force—that split-off complex within her psyche—to brush against the will of God or the Self, He was involving Himself in the struggle. The ensuing dramatic opposition between Satan and God could, as in Job's case, be instrumental in bringing shadowy and vitiated subliminal matters into consciousness, thereby paving the way for redemption. Under such circumstances, Satan, as activator, would no longer be considered evil, but rather a positive and deeply spiritual agent—a "divine being" (ibid., p. 76). As such, Yentl/Anshel's drama takes on numinous proportions, becoming an expression of an inner process leading to the birth of a new consciousness.

Luminosity in Darkness

After Avigdor married the domineering Peshe, a woman whose life was focused on material things rather than on human relationships, all went from bad to worse. When he complained of Peshe's loathsome character (shrew, miser, nagger, materialist) to Yentl/Anshel, the latter would simply list Avigdor's virtues (height, manliness, wit, erudition) and respond: "If I were a woman and married to you, I'd know how to appreciate you." Avigdor's sorrow reached such proportions at times that his "speech was incoherent, like that of a man possessed."

Yentl/Anshel also felt agony at her projected marriage to Hadass:

> Many times each day Anshel warned herself that what she was about to do was sinful, mad, an act of utter depravity. She was entangling both Hadass and herself in a chain of deception and committing so many transgressions that she would never be able to do penance. One lie followed another . . . she was in the grip of a power she could not resist.

Despite her distress, her ethics had become so distorted that she decided to go through with the marriage because she "could not bring herself to destroy Hadass's illusory happiness" by canceling the wedding. Only when Avigdor and Yentl/Anshel met twice a day to study the Talmud did they find momentary release from their misery.

The wedding date was set about the time of Hanukkah. Yentl/Anshel allowed herself to be outfitted for the event, resorting to all kinds of subterfuges. So adept had she become in this domain that she felt herself capable of doing the impossible. "Fooling the community had become a game" for her. Would the truth ever surface? Although admittedly a transgressor, she justified her conduct by arguing that "her soul thirsted to study Torah"; thus must she commit such an infraction.

Why were the nuptials set at the time of Hanukkah? The Hanukkah festival commemorates the rededication of the Second Temple by Judah the Maccabee in 165 B.C.E., on the third anniversary of its desecration by Antiochus Epiphanes (1 Maccabees 4:59). The festival lasted eight days, the Talmudic legend tells us, because the pure oil found burning in the temple, although sufficient for but a single day, miraculously burned for eight days.

One of the most important features of the Hanukkah celebration consists of the kindling of the eight-branched menorah, or candelabrum, from a light placed in a ninth socket (*shammash*). The menorah represented the "lights of holiness," a manifestation of the spiritual light given by God to Moses on Mt. Sinai and thus the "lights of the commandment" as well as the primordial light. In Exodus we read:

> And thou shalt make a candlestick of pure gold: of beaten work shall the candlestick be made: his shaft, and his branches, his bowls, his knops, and his flowers, shall be of the same (25:31). And thou shalt make the seven lamps thereof: and they shall light the lamps thereof, that they may give light over against it (25:36).

That Yentl/Anshel's marriage took place before the holiday commemorating the miracle of the lights, thereby diminishing the role of darkness, suggested in her case the symbolic birth of increased understanding. The interplay of light and darkness—the dazzling luminosities cast throughout the synagogue, representing enlightenment of the soul—was particularly significant in Eastern

Europe at this time, when only the wealthiest groups could afford electricity.

Following the marriage of Yentl/Anshel and Hadass and the performance of the "virtue dance," bride and groom were "led separately to the marriage chamber. The wedding attendants instructed the couple in the proper conduct and enjoined them to 'be fruitful and multiply.' " Early the following morning, the bride's mother and her group of ladies entered the marriage chamber, found traces of blood on the sheets, and "the company grew merry and began kissing and congratulating the bride."

Singer omits all details concerning the sexual activities in the bridal chamber. With tongue in cheek, however, he writes: "Anshel had found a way to deflower the bride. Hadass in her innocence was unaware that things weren't quite as they should have been. She was already deeply in love with Anshel."

Months passed. The marriage seemingly was a happy one. The only dark cloud on the horizon was the fact that Hadass had not become pregnant. Avigdor's relationship with his wife, Peshe, however, had grown impossible. Because she had refused to give Avigdor enough to eat, Yentl/Anshel not only brought him a buckwheat cake daily, but invited him to eat with her and Hadass.

Avigdor, refusing categorically to have a child with Peshe, preferred, he said, to "act like Onan, or, as the Gemara translates it: he threshed on the inside and cast his seed without." Of the biblical Onan, who refused to honor his father's command to inseminate his brother's widow, Tamar, it is written: "and when he went into his brother's wife, that he spilled it on the ground, lest that he should give seed to his brother" (Genesis 38:9).

Avigdor's autoerotic activities, which brought him to a climax, was a means toward an end and not intended to provoke fantasies which would then result in orgasm (or, psychologically, the discharge of instinctual tension). Had he not been deprived of love, had he been able to marry Hadass, his sexual practices would have been both normal and harmonious. "Oh, Anshel, how I envy you," Avigdor confessed. "There's no reason for envying me," was the reply. "Everyone has troubles of his own."

As the weeks and months passed, Yentl/Anshel was experiencing increasing torment. "Lying with Hadass and deceiving her had become more and more painful. Hadass's love and tenderness shamed her." Life's complexities were also growing intolerable. When, for example, on Friday afternoons the townspeople went to

the baths to welcome the Sabbath in purity and cleanliness, Yentl/
Anshel had to keep finding excuses for not going along. The townspeople grew suspicious. Did he have a hidden unsightly birthmark?
Had he been improperly circumcised? And why wasn't Hadass
pregnant?

The more aware Yentl/Anshel became of her deception, the
greater was her torment. "The lie was swelling like an abscess and
one of these days it must surely burst." She understood that she
could not long continue such dissimulation.

Passover

During Passover week, it was the custom for young men to take a
trip to nearby cities to buy things they wanted or needed, such as
books, or to find new business opportunities. When Yentl/Anshel
invited the impoverished Avigdor to spend a few days at a nearby
town, Bechev, he accepted with delight.

The Passover holiday, called "the festival of freedom" because
it commemorates the exodus of the children of Israel from Egypt,
would also be auspicious for Avigdor and Yentl/Anshel. It would
mark the beginning of their liberation or rebirth—as well as of
nature's.

> The fields were turning green; storks, back from the warm coun-
> tries, sweeped across the sky in great arcs. Streams rushed toward
> the valleys. The birds chirped. The windmills turned. Spring
> flowers were beginning to bloom in the fields.

During their merry carriage ride, Yentl/Anshel told Avigdor
that she had a secret she would reveal to him when they reached
their destination. Understandably, he thought it concerned an essay
that his friend had written or some hidden treasure he had discovered. That night, after Yentl/Anshel had made certain the door of
the room they shared was locked, she said to him: "Prepare yourself
for the most incredible thing that ever was." Whereupon she confessed to being a woman and not a man. Because Avigdor burst out
laughing, Yentl said, "Then I'll get undressed." Avigdor suddenly
became nervous: "Anshel might want to practice pederasty," he
feared. When Yentl started disrobing, Avigdor turned "white, then
fiery red." So stunned was he that he began to tremble. Moments

later, he murmured: "How is it possible? I don't believe it!" Yentl answered defiantly: "Should I get undressed again?"

Even after relating her entire story to Avigdor, he still thought he was living a nightmare and that nothing she said was true. Why hadn't she told him before? "We could have . . ." No, Yentl said, attempting once again to dissimulate her real feelings for him: "I'm neither one nor the other." She revealed her secret, she told him, so that he would be able to testify at the courthouse as to her gender, after which Hadass would be granted a divorce. Avigdor would also be granted one and, finally, he and Hadass would marry.

Still Avigdor could not believe the story. Were all of their intimate conversations and their friendship delusions? Were their disputations spurious? Was Anshel a demon? "He shook himself as if to cast off a nightmare; yet that power which knows the difference between dream and reality told him it was all true."

When the two began discussing the commentaries concerning the legality of a divorce under certain conditions, their conversation became so involved that they were soon lost in Talmudic speculation: "the Torah had reunited them. Though their bodies were different, their souls were of one kind." And as they talked, "a great love for Anshel took hold of Avigdor, mixed with shame, remorse, anxiety. If I had only known this before, he said to himself." Only now did Avigdor realize that he had always longed for a wife "whose mind was not taken up with material things . . . His desire for Hadass was gone now, and he knew he would long for Yentl, but he dared not say so."

The two counted their sins in the darkness of the room, Avigdor's by association, Yentl's by design. She told him that the only reason she had married Hadass was to be near him. "You could have married me," he replied. "I wanted to study the Gemara and Commentaries with you, not darn your socks!" she answered. Again Avigdor asked: "If you're willing . . ." And she replied: "No, Avigdor. It wasn't destined to be . . . I'll live out my time as I am," she responded.

To spare Hadass greater heartache, it was decided that Yentl would not return to Lublin. Instead, she would send her a divorce by mail. This she did. So heartbroken was Hadass that she began wasting away. Why had her husband left her? She, who loved him so tenderly. The townspeople as well tried to understand the reasons for his departure. Had he been seduced or converted? Was he a demon? Had he so transgressed that he went into exile to do penance?

In time, Peshe granted Avigdor a divorce, after which he married Hadass. Everything about the wedding feast was perfect, but neither Avigdor nor Hadass knew joy. That the couple named their first child Anshel stunned the townspeople. Guesses are still forthcoming as to what had really occurred. And Singer writes with his inimitable humor:

> It is a general rule that when the grain of truth cannot be found, men will swallow great helpings of falsehood. Truth itself is often concealed in such a way that the harder you look for it, the harder it is to find.

No mention is made of Yentl's fate. Now that she had confessed her "sin" to the one person she loved and had sacrificed that love for the dazzling luminosities of the mind, her newfound purity of spirit enabled her to come to terms with what the community might look upon as her shadowy and deceptive side. But might not Yentl, as a struggling, sacrificing, and sorrowful individual who longed to develop her mind and to live as an equal among her male brethren, be looked upon as the prototype of today's woman in the world at large? Now that she had completed her rite of passage and had made her choice in full awareness of the difficulties and deceptions involved, could she not be considered one of many Yentls rising up throughout history, all somehow paving the way for the breakup of the old order? Isn't it her voice that looms strong—like Deborah's—after centuries of silence?

Note

1. Although victory over Barak's enemy followed, its fruits were far sweeter, as related in the Talmud, centuries later when Rabbi Akiva, a descendent of Sisera, Barak's foe, not only laid the foundations for the oral law, but also codified the Mishnah. Thus did former adversaries work together in the name of God (Telushkin 1991, p. 71).

Bibliography

Baron, S. W. 1964. *Russian Jew Under Tsars and Soviets*. New York: The Macmillan Co.

Goldin, J. 1957. *The Living Talmud*. New York: New American Library.

Gottlieb, F. 1989. *The Lamp of God*. London: Jason Aronson Inc.

Harding, E. 1971. *Psychic Energy*. Princeton, N.J.: Princeton University Press.

Jacobi, Y. 1959. *Complex Archetype Symbol in the Psychology of C. G. Jung*. Translated by R. Manheim. Princeton, N.J.: Princeton University Press.

Jung, C. G. 1960. *The Psychogenesis of Mental Disease*. *CW*, vol. 3. Translated by R. F. C. Hull. New York: Pantheon Books.

————. 1971. *Psychological Types*. A revision by R. F. C. Hull of the translation by H. G. Baynes. Princeton, N.J.: Princteon University Press.

————. 1976. *The Visions Seminars*, vol. II. Zurich: Spring Publications.

————. 1984. *Seminar on Dream Analysis*. Edited by W. McGuire. Princeton, N.J.: Princeton University Press.

Kluger, R. S. 1967. *Satan in the Old Testament*. Evanston, Ill.: Northwestern University Press.

Kravitz, N. 1972. *3000 Years of Hebrew Literature*. Chicago: The Swallow Press.

Reis, P. 1991. *Through the Goddess*. New York: Continuum.

Singer, I. B. 1991. *The Collected Stories*. New York: Farrar, Straus, Giroux.

Steinsaltz, Rabbi A., trans. 1989. *The Talmud: A Reference Guide*. New York: Random House.

Telushkin, J. 1991. *Jewish Legacy*. New York: William Morrow and Co.

von Franz, M.-L. 1978. *Projection and Re-Collection in Jungian Psychology*. London: Open Court.

————. 1974. *Shadow and Evil in Fairy Tales*. Zurich: Spring Publications.

Index

masculine principle, 121, 132
Matthew, Book of, 64
meditation, 65, 67, 70–71, 74,
    79–81, 87, 111
Meir, Rabbi, 146
menorah, 163
mercury, 90
Mesmer, 126
metanoia, 115
metaphor, 42
Middle Ages, 8
Miriam, 82, 140
Mishnah, 1, 145–146, 148–149, 153n.
moon, as symbol, 120, 125, 129,
    131–132, 136–137
Moses, 4, 10, 35, 49–50, 53, 55n.,
    79, 90, 114, 128, 131, 140,
    144–146, 163
Mother Earth (Earth Mother), 19, 26,
    116
    see also Great Mother
mountain, as symbol, 117–118,
    130–131
mysticism, 38–39, 43, 66, 73, 75,
    78–79, 81, 89–90
    ecstatic, 4, 41
    Hebrew, 38–39, 71, 101
myth, 2–4, 11, 19, 23, 49, 90, 103,
    116
    werewolf, 23

Nachman, Rabbi Ben Simhah, 3, 5,
    97, 99–103, 105–106, 109–111,
    116, 118–119, 132
Narodniki, 67
Nathan, the Prophet, 8
Nebuchadnezzar, 142
Neumann, E., 18, 25–27, 130
New Testament, 64
numbers, 42–43, 54, 70–71
    see also gematria, numerology
    forty, 128
    seven, 56, 88
Numbers, Book of, 4, 8, 10, 13–15,
    30, 35, 43, 92, 128–129, 144
numerology, 80
numinosum, 1, 65, 147

Odysseus, 11–13, 20, 23
Old Testament, 43, 64
Onan, 164
Origen, 75
Orpheus, 12

Ovid, 11, 129

Pan Ku, *see* giant
Paracelsus, 40
participation mystique, 130
Parzival, 11, 21, 152–153
Passover, 4, 44, 47, 49, 165
Pausanius, 23
pearl, as symbol, 118
persona, 13, 15–16, 151, 157–158
Petronius, 23
Plato, 19, 82
Pliny, 23, 74, 129
Popul Vuh, 124
prayer, 65, 67, 70–71, 79, 81, 87,
    132, 145
    as transformation ritual, 50
prima materia, 116
projection, 5, 8, 22, 24–25, 27, 31,
    34, 41, 51, 57, 62, 77, 94, 98, 102,
    108–109, 111, 133
    double, 23
Proust, 103
Proverbs of Solomon, 8, 18, 78
psyche, 1–2, 13, 15, 20, 24, 26–27,
    43, 50, 52, 57, 64, 71–72, 80,
    83–87, 89, 94, 98, 103, 105–106,
    108, 111, 121, 124, 126–127,
    129–131, 134–135, 140, 147–148,
    153, 155, 157–160, 162
    and soma, 71, 77, 80
    child, 123
    collective, 23, 29, 89
    Hebrew, 147
psychology, depth, viii
psychotherapy, 63
Purim, 55n.
Purusha, *see* giant
Puységur, Marquis de, 126
Pythagoras, 71

Read, J., 56n.
redemption, 75, 108
Reis, P., 143
religion, 103, 120

Samuel, Book of, 8, 64, 133
Sandys, J. E., 40
Sanhedrin, 45
Sarah, 140
Satan, 140, 160–162
Saul, 64
Schaya, L., 110